Eric
Hosking's
OWLS

Eric Hosking's
OWLS

ERIC HOSKING
OBE, Hon. FRPS, FIIP

with Dr Jim Flegg
BSc, ARCS, PhD

Foreword by Ian Prestt
Director of the Royal Society for the Protection of Birds

Mermaid Books

First published in Great Britain in Mermaid Books by Pelham Books Ltd
44 Bedford Square London WC1B 3DP
1985
Original edition published by Pelham Books Ltd in 1982

British Library Cataloguing in Publication Data
Hosking, Eric
  Eric Hosking's owls.
  1. Owls
  I. Title
  598'.97   QL696.S8

ISBN: 0 7207 1601 2

Printed and bound in Spain by Printer IGSA
Sant Vicenç dels Horts   Barcelona   D.L.B. 715-1985

Contents

To my grandchildren –
Iain, James, Elizabeth and Charlotte

Opposite title page: *Banking as it cuts between the trees on the way to its nest hole, a Barn Owl brings home the first meal of the evening.*

Contents page spread: *Wings spread in heraldic posture almost like an egret, a male Snowy Owl lands alongside the owlets, a young rabbit in his talons.*

PUBLISHER'S NOTE
Readers should note that the companion volume to this book, Eric Hosking's Birds, *which is mentioned throughout the text, was published in the United States of America by Coward McCann under the title* A Passion For Birds.

Foreword

by Ian Prestt,

Director of the Royal Society for the Protection of Birds

I clearly recall my first meeting with Eric Hosking. I was a relatively new boy at boarding school and a recently awakened general interest in natural history was beginning to develop into something more purposeful through my membership of the long established and very active school natural history society. On this particular evening we had been invited to attend what would be my first professional lecture on birds which was to be given by a young man called Eric Hosking. Even at this early stage in his career and with the major part of his professional life still ahead of him he was given advanced billing as one of our leading bird photographers. Thus it was with considerable excitement and anticipation that we arranged ourselves in the school hall, where the huge lantern projector with its brass fittings had been prepared to receive the heavy glass slides. And what a fascinating occasion it proved to be.

Most of the lecture was devoted to the stone curlew in the East Anglian Brecks, a species and habitat then unknown to me as a northerner. But of even greater significance for me than the superb portraits we were shown of this strange, large-eyed, leggy bird in its sparsely vegetated, flinty breeding grounds, was the insight into the techniques employed and what could be learnt through them. He revealed such wonders as the effectiveness of the bird's plumage in protecting the incubating bird, the division of parental responsibilities and the behaviour during changeover at the nest, the hatching of the young and their reaction to danger. By the careful construction of a simple hide and the exercise of a little patience he demonstrated how a whole new insight into the fascinating life of birds becomes possible.

I know I was not alone that evening in finding inspiration and a new sense of purpose from what I saw and heard. Eric Hosking's love of his subject, his attention to detail and striving for perfection were all clearly communicated. Since then, literally hundreds of thousands of people must have had their interest kindled through attending his lectures and reading his many books. This early appreciation by him that high-quality photographs accompanied by an informative text, whether written or spoken, form one of the most potent means of introducing people to the wonder and beauty of birdlife accounts for his considerable contribution to wildlife conservation. This achievement was acknowledged by his election as one of the small number of Vice Presidents of the Royal Society for the Protection of Birds. That a fellow Vice President was the late Charles

Tunnicliffe, one of Britain's leading bird painters, simply serves to underline the debt that conservationists owe to artists such as these.

Particularly when presented in book form, the value of even the finest photographs can be considerably enhanced when supported by a good text. The choice of Jim Flegg as author for *Eric Hosking's Owls* has added immeasurably to its worth. Like Eric Hosking, Jim Flegg manages to combine the enthusiasm of the amateur with the discipline of the professional – a factor which must have influenced his appointment to his previous position as Director of the British Trust for Ornithology, a research body particularly admired in other countries for the way it brings together the professional and amateur ornithologist. Increasingly Jim Flegg is following the tradition established by Eric Hosking of sharing his interest with others through lectures, radio broadcasts and publications.

It came as no surprise to me that the volume chosen to follow *Eric Hosking's Birds* was one devoted to owls. From an early stage in his career, owls have held a fascination for Eric and one of his most celebrated portraits shows a Barn Owl in heraldic pose. An interest in owls is not confined to specialists and however uninformed or disinterested a person may be about birds in general one can be quite sure they will recognize an owl. Children have them as cuddly toys and they appear in nursery rhymes, children's books and plays. In adult literature they commonly feature, somewhat in contradiction, as figures either of stupidity or great wisdom and are not infrequently selected as the voice of the puritanical moralizer. No doubt their dumpy, fluffy appearance, flat, rather human face and lazy or unruffled behaviour in daylight (whichever way you interpret it) accounts for all this.

In reality owls represent a superbly adapted animal group with exceptional powers of vision and hearing enabling them to fly or hunt on the darkest night. They are also a most successful group, having radiated out to form many species occupying widely differing niches in different parts of the world and include huge birds such as the Snowy Owl of Arctic wastes, tiny burrowing owls in the desert and fish-feeding owls in Africa. The familiar Barn Owl of the British farm is found across the world and no fewer than thirty-four geographical races of it have been described.

Owls have represented something of a challenge to both biologists and photographers – how do you study something you can't see but which can see you? This 'turning of the tables' after dark to the advantage of the owl was only too tragically illustrated when Eric lost an eye to a Tawny Owl he was photographing. I suppose most of us like a challenge: I recall at another school lecture this theme being developed by one of the pioneers of recording bird song, Ludwig Koch, who was determined, despite primitive equipment, to record the aerial song of the skylark because a newspaper article had reported that it would be impossible! Likewise Eric has persevered, although it seems a long way from the present portraits obtained with the latest electronic flash sensitive to an insect to the early days when he had to listen for the scratch of talons on the tree bark as his cue to fire the shutter. Much of the early biological information about the flight and food of owls was revealed through photography.

In recent years Eric has been joined by his son David, whose enthusiasm and ability in the field of wildlife photography are following in the Hosking tradition. It is good to see examples of his work appearing in this book.

I am particularly conscious of the debt that conservationists owe to people like Eric Hosking and Jim Flegg. If our birdlife and other animals and wild plants are to be saved it is vital to gain widespread support from the public, both in the cities and countryside. The skilful use of photography and imaginative texts have played a most important role in this and will continue to do so in the future. I welcome this new work as a further major contribution and have no doubt of its success and trust there will be many more like it to follow.

Preface

Let me begin by saying that I am a wildlife photographer not a writer so I am full of admiration for Dr Jim Flegg who has so willingly and so vividly written the text. He is a first-rate ornithologist as I know from field expeditions I have had with him to India and Nepal. Now he brings his expertise to this book on owls and I am so grateful to him.

Although full of admiration for men like Ian Prestt, who have devoted their lives to the protection of wildlife, it was with some hesitation that he was approached to write the Foreword. He is the Director of the Royal Society for the Protection of Birds with its huge 300,000-plus membership and he is an extremely busy man. However, like most busy men he found the time to take on yet another job. It made me feel very humble to read his words and to realize how much I have influenced young people during their impressionable years. Indeed I am sorry that the intense pressures of lecturing forced me to give it up entirely in 1963.

Looking through this collection of photographs of owls, taken over the past fifty-two years, makes me appreciate how much I owe to so many friends. It would be nice to mention them all by name but this would make a long catalogue. However, there are some who helped me so much it would be ungracious not to name them. Top of the list must come my son David, now in partnership with me, who has not only taken quite a number of the photographs in this book but also has helped in very many other ways. He is making full use of all the modern techniques, ideas and equipment and is now leaving his father far behind. As always, my wife Dorothy has assisted me not only in carrying heavy equipment but also, on expeditions at home and abroad, has coped with all the chores that inevitably crop up, leaving me free to concentrate on photography.

Naturally it is much more rewarding, exciting and challenging to photograph animals in an entirely free and wild state but this is not always possible and there is a limit to what one can achieve in a single lifetime. Owls are found in almost every country of the world, some with very limited distribution and so rare that to disturb them might even prejudice their breeding potential. Time and expense make it impossible to travel to the far ends of the earth to locate some of the rarer species. Therefore quite a lot of the owls have been photographed in captivity. A full account of how this is done is given in the chapter entitled 'Colourful Birds and Zoo Photography' in the companion volume *Eric Hosking's Birds* (Pelham Books, 1979).

I am grateful to Margaret and Bill Beer for allowing us to photograph the wild Tawny Owls they had been feeding for many years and for kindly inviting us to spend so many nights at their home. I must also thank Paul Morrison for introducing me to this charming couple. Phillip Glasier and his family have always put down the red carpet and given us a great deal of their time whenever we have visited the Falconry Centre in Newent, Gloucestershire. In the same way Bernard Sayers must be thanked and it was a joy to photograph his immaculate owls in Essex. Len Hill at Birdland, Bourton-on-the-Water, has among his marvellous collection, several fine owls which he allowed us to portray in our portable studio. Peter Bloomfield and Bill Timmis were enthusiastic for us to get good pictures of the owls at Chester Zoo and we are grateful to them and also to Dr Michael Brambell, the director. Since then Bill has moved on to Harewood Bird Gardens in Yorkshire and we have been able to visit these lovely gardens on two occasions. We used to spend a lot of time photographing the splendid collection of owls at London Zoo and would like to thank Peter Olney, curator of birds, for all his help.

While in New Zealand and Australia in 1981 we were treated like royalty. We had only to mention the name of something we wished to photograph and it was produced. To Geoff Moon in New Zealand, Donald and Mollie Trounson, Peter and Pat Slater, Bruce and Margaret Kubbere, Don and Betty Lawson, and David Fleay in Australia we owe a great debt. Peter Davey in Kenya and Peter Steyn in Rhodesia (as it was then but now, of course, Zimbabwe) gave us great assistance. One of the highlights of our visit to the Seychelles was meeting Jeff Watson and we shall never forget how, after dark and with the aid of a tape recording he had made of their calls, he brought the extremely rare Bare-legged Scops Owl to within a few feet of the camera.

Back home we would like to thank Donald Smith for letting us use his Short-eared Owl hide in Ayrshire; Roger Hosking for making it possible to take the Barn Owl sequences in flight on his farm in Devon; Bobby Tulloch up in Fetlar, Shetland, without whose help we could never have obtained the photographs of the first breeding pair of Snowy Owls recorded in the British Isles; John Hawkins who not only gave us accommodation while staying in Shropshire but also found so many nests for us; and Mike Gill of the Game Conservancy who located and arranged for us to photograph the tree-nesting Barn Owls in Hampshire.

We are also grateful to Richard Morris for sending us the remarkable photograph of the Eagle Owl taken in 1854 in Clifton Zoo, Bristol, by John Dillwyn Llewellyn, who was cousin by marriage of the great pioneer of photography, Fox Talbot.

We would like to take this opportunity of thanking the Olympus Optical Company, and particularly their British managing director, Barry Taylor, for all the great kindness they have shown us. We have no hesitation in saying that Olympus cameras, lenses and flash, together with their other equipment, have made our photography of owls in recent years so much more simple than it was even a few years ago.

We would like to wish Eric Marriott every possible happiness in his retirement. It was he who asked us to do this book while he was managing director of Pelham Books and his enthusiasm was a marvellous stimulant to us. Lesley Gowers and Patricia Walters have done marvels with the production and lay-out and we would like them to know just how much we appreciate their hard work.

Without all those mentioned above, and many others, this book could never have come into being.

ERIC HOSKING
October, 1981

The Fascination of Owls

One of my earliest owl photographs: a Suffolk Barn Owl carrying a rat that I did not know was there until I saw the developed image. The old-style flash bulb burned too slowly to arrest the movement in the rat's tail. Opposite: The Tawny Owl that caused me to lose an eye clambers awkwardly back into her nest.

'There can be no doubt that my favourites in the whole world of birds are the owls, those amazing birds of the night.' That is what I wrote in *Eric Hosking's Birds*, published by Pelham Books, and this volume, devoted entirely to the owls, is the logical outcome. I hope that through its pages, at least some of my own interest and enthusiasm will be caught by the reader.

In almost every form of wildlife photography it is possible to see the object you are taking, but most owls are nocturnal which presents problems because you cannot see them to focus the camera! Even with the crepuscular owls, which are about when the light is fading, you cannot see them clearly enough to obtain critical focus. But perhaps it is because you are working in the dark so often that owl photography is so exciting.

The very characteristic heart-shaped face of a Barn Owl, very much the Hosking family favourite owl, peering out of a nest hole in a hollow tree awaiting the arrival of her mate with food. Notice how electronic flash gives pin-point accuracy to detail.

When working on a pair of Barn Owls in Suffolk many years ago I was able to focus on the nesting hole before it was dark. As I waited for one of the owls to return it got darker and darker, and as it did so my imagination ran riot until I was certain the bird was sitting there waiting for me to fire the flash. I did so, and in the momentary light could see that my eyes were playing me false and realized that it was far better to use my ears. Owls are silent fliers, but somehow the youngsters knew, down in their nesting hole, when the adult was about and started to make a curious churring noise. A moment later the faint sound of claws contacting the bark could be heard at the mouth of the hole. I then sucked air in between my lips to draw the bird's attention and make it look round and face the camera as the flash was fired. Even with this technique I had far more failures than successes, but the best proved to be one of the most famous photographs I have ever taken. Of course I did not realize it at the time and only when I had developed the negative did I see that not only was the owl perfectly shown but in its bill was a rat. I was so excited I raced down the stairs two at a time with the wet negative in my hand shouting to my mother 'Look, it's got a rat in its bill!' That was forty-six years ago, and since then owl photography has changed completely.

Today we just let the owls photograph themselves and sometimes even go to bed while they do so. In the summer of 1979, my son David and I were shown the nest of a pair of Barn Owls in the attic of an old, derelict building in Dorset. By careful watching we saw that they flew in through a hole in the roof, over a partition wall and down to the owlets. We were able to fit a photo-electric cell, for automatically taking the photographs, on the floor pointing up to a lamp unit fixed to a rafter. We knew the owls would have to fly through the light beam and by so doing, interrupt the circuit which activates the camera shutter and with it the two high-speed lamp units, and then the motor-drive to wind on the film. The camera was erected and focussed on the spot, the flash lamps adjusted so that they would fire while the owl was in flight. As we were using a motor-drive on the Olympus OM-2n camera, thirty-six exposures could be made without our having to go near the camera. Meticulous care was taken to see that everything was just right. As it was getting late, on this fine night in June, we decided to go to bed in our Auto-Sleeper parked about a hundred yards away.

At five the next morning David hurried to the site and found that all thirty-six exposures had gone through the camera – thirty-six super photographs of Barn Owls in flight! We just could not wait to see the results so I drove to Kodak in Hertfordshire to get the film processed. Meanwhile David telephoned to warn them I was coming. The excitement became intense – there should be eighteen cracking pictures of the owl flying towards the camera and a similar number of it flying away. After five long hours the results were handed to me, and with trembling fingers I looked at them. A nice shot of a wall but no sign of an owl; the second the same, and the third, and so on right through the thirty-six! What had gone wrong? With a fairly powerful magnifying glass I examined the transparencies more carefully. There were the culprits, right bang in the centre – a mosquito in one, a tiny beetle in another, in the third a small clothes moth, and so on. The photo-electric cell was too sensitive. We re-set it and tried again, and one of the results is shown in this book.

In 1937 I was attacked by a Tawny Owl and lost my left eye, and because of this every time I hear a Tawny call, as they do round our home in London, the hair on the back of my neck rises and queer shivers run down my spine. So when we were invited to visit Mr and Mrs Beer at their bungalow in Buckinghamshire to photograph a pair that came down to take bait I was terribly thrilled. The bait was put on a tree stump close to the door which was left open so that we could watch. The photo-electric cell, flash and camera were erected. The owls did not come until it was dark so all we saw was a blinding flash. Each time the bait was taken another was put out, and usually five or six went before we packed up at about midnight. When the Tawnies had large young the amount of bait taken increased, and one night no less than twenty-five disappeared, far more than the young could possibly have eaten. We suspected the adults were hiding it, perhaps in the nesting hole. That night they were so anxious to take the food that before David had a chance to replace it and get out of the way the owl swooped down, taking not only its own photograph but David's as well.

15

Before my son David had time to move away after placing bait on the stump, this hungry Tawny Owl swooped through the photo-electric beam and triggered both flash and shutter, catching them both in the act!

Whenever we make plans to visit a new country we find out what species of owl will be found there and what chances there might be of photographing them. Unfortunately it often happens that there is just not time to go searching for a nest or to erect a hide from which to take the photographs and it is far more practicable to visit collections or other places where owls are kept in aviaries. Thus it was when we visited Australia during the spring of 1981 that we discovered there was just one place where all eight species could be seen. This was at Burleigh in Queensland, not far from Brisbane, and it was owned by a remarkable elderly gentleman of some eighty years, David Fleay. He was utterly devoted to his animals and, I believe, the only person who has ever succeeded in rearing that curious egg-laying mammal the duck-billed platypus. At first he did not receive us at all enthusiastically because he imagined we wanted to interfere with his owls and he was not prepared to have them caught up or handled in any way. But when he saw I was an owl fanatic and was prepared to take photographs through the wire netting of the aviaries, he

16

This time the Tawny approaches the bait from a different angle, and clearly has both eyes intently fixed on its target.

thawed out and we had the most interesting and delightful conversation. He worries because he can see no future for his fine collection and is getting too old to give them all the care and devotion they need. Surely such a unique collection which has such great educational value should be run by the State for the benefit of the local people? Here for the first time in our lives we saw the endemic Powerful Owl, as well as the Rufous and Barking Owls, and we spent a wonderful day trying to photograph them.

Obviously it is much more exciting, challenging and rewarding to photograph the owls in their natural habitat, free and wild. But there are about 130 species found through the whole of the world and it would be impossible, in a single life-time, to locate them all. Thus a number of the photographs were taken under controlled conditions in our portable studio which is described in detail in *Eric Hosking's Birds*.

Just a word about the equipment we use to photograph owls as it may save readers the trouble of writing fruitless letters to us. There is no commercially built

17

The Rufous Owl, one of David Fleay's fine collection of owls at Burleigh, Queensland. The habitats of the Rufous Owl are the rainforests and savannah woodlands in the north of Australia and in New Guinea. Rather small, at 45 cm (18 ins), the Rufous Owl makes up in aggressiveness what it lacks in size. This captive bird is ballooning out its feathers in intimidation. In the wild, Rufous Owls will not tolerate other owls in their hunting and breeding areas. Their range of prey, centring on the tree-living opossums, is much the same as that of their larger relatives and underlines their hunting prowess.

18

My favourite Barn Owl photograph. This 'one-in-a-million' shot has caught the bird in an heraldic, even angelic, pose. All its features are crisply displayed, even down to the short tail-length of the vole it is bringing back to its youngsters. This photograph has been reproduced more often than any other and must be one of the best-known bird photographs in the world.

high-speed flash equipment on the market that will give the power and the short duration flash we need. Ours have been made specially for us, and this has been done privately so we cannot recommend a manufacturer. One major problem is that to obtain adequate power we need high voltages, and these can be very dangerous, indeed lethal, if not used carefully by someone who knows what he is doing. Another way is to use several computer flash guns all linked together at the same flash duration, in this way building up the light output. However, we feel sure that such is the rapid development of all things photographic and electronic that it will not be long before appropriate equipment is commercially available.

19

The Exploits of Owls

Owls in history

Owls are clearly recognizable as owls – by anybody, young or old, interested in birds or not. This may seem an absurd statement, but it has meaning: the 'man in the street' can easily conjure up a mental picture of an owl, whereas he would be hard pressed to describe the far more common dunnock that frequents his garden every day, or the colourful jay or even such a spectacular bird as the gannet.

Perhaps largely because owls are so readily identified, we should not be too surprised that they feature greatly in our daily lives in many ways. They occur commonly (almost as often as the robin) on our Christmas cards and they are perhaps the most widely used bird subject for ornaments. Dorothy, my wife, will testify to this as we have several hundred pottery, wood, stone or metal owls of all sizes in the house. Owls must be one of the first birds to be recognized by babies, if only because they feature regularly on the mobiles that swing over most babies' cots today. When the child grows older, he has owl cuddly toys, and reads nursery rhymes like

> *The owl and the pussycat went to sea*
> *In a beautiful pea-green boat.*

Owls have featured regularly in the printed word, in story and in verse, for at least as long as printing has existed. *The Owl and the Nightingale* dates from the thirteenth century, and there are numerous references in Shakespeare. Sometimes the owl is nominated as a messenger of ill-omen, as in *Julius Caesar* and *Macbeth*, but in others, like *Love's Labour's Lost*, the Tawny Owl is portrayed in a more kindly light and, incidentally, more accurately from a natural history point of view. Even earlier, owls are amongst the birds featuring (perhaps with a little assistance from translators) in the Old Testament of the Bible. Leviticus XI, for example, refers to 'the little owl, and the cormorant, and the great owl' as birds that 'shall not be eaten.'

No worthwhile alchemist, magician or witch in fairy tale or fable would be without his or her owl. King Arthur's magician, Merlin, is often depicted with an owl as his 'familiar', and owls are regarded almost universally as birds of wisdom. An

Opposite: The origin of the 'cuddly toy' owl? Few young birds could be so appealing as these young Tengmalm's Owls. Although out of the nest for some air and wing exercises, the amount of down still remaining indicates that they are some days from fledging.

21

Left: *Better known for its pictorial representation of a gift of wine to the King of Persia, this Greek vase or jug, dating from about the 4th century BC, also depicts a prominent owl. Although clearly recognizable as an owl, it would be a brave man who would put a name to it.* Right: *So superbly sculpted and so realistic is this archaic Greek owl found at the Acropolis in Athens that we can feel happy with an identification as a Little Owl (Athene) – held in sacred reverence by the citizens of Athens.*

excellent example (although his spelling is rather weak) is Wol in the *Winnie the Pooh* books, but even sober scientists follow suit when we see the Little Owl named after Athene, the Greek goddess of wisdom. The Little Owl, which must have been common in the area, was the sacred owl of the city of Athens and featured on some of the earliest local coins.

This association of man with owls is very deep rooted in our history. In Palaeolithic times, when earth was in the grip of one of the ice ages, early European man was forced to seek shelter in cave systems. In France, the extraordinarily beautiful cave paintings (for example at Lascaux) that these early men left depict many of the animals of the time in excellent detail. With unbelievable artistry, they have left a pictorial record of much of the natural history of their times. This includes an easily recognized family portrait of a pair of Snowy Owls with their young, amazingly similar in composition to those I photographed on Fetlar (Shetland Isles) (see pages 4–5 and 94–96) with such excitement so many centuries later.

Despite the strictures of Judaic law that I have mentioned, the archaelogists can tell us, having searched through the remains of kitchen scraps on middens dating back to Neolithic times, that Snowy Owls featured in the diet of these early men.

22

This is probably the first photograph ever taken of an owl. It is of a Spotted Eagle Owl (note the characteristically disproportionately small head), an African species photographed in captivity in Clifton Zoo, Bristol, by John Dillwyn Llewellyn in 1854.

This is also true today in remote Eskimo settlements where living off the land is the only way of life. These Eskimos have immortalized the owl in their traditional soapstone carvings whittled during the long cold hours of winter darkness.

On the other side of the globe, those fabulous rock artists, the Aborigines of Arnhem Land in north Australia, have painted a more abstract 'owl man' with clearly recognizable owl features, perhaps symbolic of the spirit world that has always obsessed them so.

Is it only because we can identify owls so easily that they are so popular? Our attitude to them is somewhat ambivalent: often we positively like them and admire their knowledge, but at the same time there is an element of fear, and sometimes a link with ill fortune. I think there must be more to it than that. Perhaps their upright, manikin-like stance helps us to liken owls to the human form. Their large heads and rather human faces, with marked cheeks, large forward-facing eyes and sometimes ears in the form of tufts of feathers, would strengthen this association, and it could be regarded as a natural step to attribute to them our own brain capability and thus wisdom.

Although owls are highly specialized for their way of life, having (for example) well-developed eyes and ears for hunting in poor light conditions, there is nothing, anatomically, about their brains that would support the view that they possess more wisdom than any other bird.

Few men, in ancient *or* modern times, could fail to be impressed by the startlingly ferocious appearance of the bright-orange eyes and fearsome face pattern of the huge Eagle Owl, or frightened by after-dark glimpses of a ghostly white Barn Owl, silent in flight but with an awful shriek of a call. Hence, perhaps, the origin of one side of the owls-and-man story. For the other, it is easily possible to see how soft-plumaged, dark-eyed, apparently cuddly owls, like the Tawny Owl, could give rise to the favourable impressions we humans have of likeable owls, and particularly when they do good by eliminating our vermin like rats and mice.

The fossil record
One of the most informative aspects of the study of any group of creatures, but at the same time most tantalizing and frustrating, is their fossil record. Many small, delicate creatures leave little or no permanent remains that can be fossilized, and so are just not represented. For larger creatures with robust bones, so much depends on chance – when, where, and why they died – that there are always gaps in the fossil record, often at what would appear to be a crucial time, hence the frustration.

Only in certain circumstances will good fossils form: the prime requirement is a lack of disturbance. Thus an ideal situation would be where an owl, let us say, accidentally became stuck in soft mud by a lakeside while drinking. After its death, the flesh rotted away from the bones, and as the level of the lake rose, freshly sedimenting mud covered the skeleton. Over the passage of millions of years, that mud gradually hardened to rock, as did the bones of the owl, and a fossil was formed.

The history of the earth can, in a way, be reassembled from these fossil remains. There are a number of clearly demarcated periods in geological time, often associated with various climatic phases in the earth's development. Palaeontologists have given names to these periods, or epochs, the first being the Cambrian, starting about 500 million years ago. It is tempting to imagine these periods as represented by the layers of rock (complete with the fossils of some of the animals and plants) laid down at the time, rather like the various layers of an onion, with the oldest layer innermost in the earth's crust. So turbulent has been the earth's geological history that we must modify this simple idea, and imagine the various movements and the volcanic eruptions that have crumpled these rock skins as if they were paper, punching holes in some strata and standing others on end. Despite this upheaval, geologists can identify and date the rock layers with adequate precision.

The oldest fossil remains of a backboned animal are fish scales from the Ordovician period, about 400 million years ago. During the Devonian period (about 300 million years ago) the first traces of forests appear, together with the first animals capable of some form of dry-land existence, the lung fish and amphibians. Reptiles appeared over 200 million years ago, and for the next 100 million years dominated the scene. It is thought that from some of these reptiles, the earliest birds developed. There is no detailed evidence of the stages through which these reptiles

Although looking, and in many ways behaving, much like the Little Owl, this Burrowing Owl is placed in a genus of its own – Speotyto – a genus with a long ancestry stretching back through the fossil records.

passed in their general evolution towards birds – as I said, the fossil record is aggravatingly incomplete. Nonetheless, by the Jurassic period, some 150 million years ago, the earliest bird-like creature, called *Archaeopteryx*, appeared complete with feathers but with a long, fleshy tail like a lizard's – although the tail, too, was covered in feathers. *Archaeopteryx* was probably only able to scramble about in trees and to make short gliding flights.

By the Cretaceous period (60 million years ago) bird development was proceeding apace, and there were some birds in existence that can easily be related to others alive today, mostly in the diver and grebe families. Again, fossil records are scanty, not least because by the very nature of flight, demanding a lightweight skeleton, birds were destined not to leave many good fossils.

Although there are earlier fossil remains which *might* be of owls or their forerunners, the first positively identifiable owl remains date from about 50 million years ago, in the Eocene period. These were found in North America, and represent five species, all now extinct, in a primitive family called the Protostrigidae. The next seven species to be found came from the Oligocene period some 25 million or more years ago, and were discovered in France. They are placed in the modern family Strigidae, and include two which resemble quite closely owls alive today. One belongs to the genus *Bubo* – the Eagle Owls – and the other is very similar to the Short-eared Owl in the genus *Asio*.

Between 25 and 10 million years ago (the Miocene period) the other modern owl family – the Tytonidae – comes to light with five species of early Barn Owls from

25

Left: *The tawny frogmouth of Australia is a nocturnal hunter. Its very owl-like appearance is slightly misleading and probably the result of what is called parallel evolution. Some taxonomists suspect that way back in time, owls and frogmouths may have had common ancestors.* Right: *The nightjar, a specialist insect feeding bird that, like many owls, hunts at night and relies on good camouflage to remain undisturbed during the day. Though adaptations to nocturnal life (like large eyes) could have arisen independently, there is evidence from studies of egg-white proteins that owls and nightjars may have come from a common origin in the distant past.*

France. This was clearly the time when the daylight hunters, the eagles, hawks and falcons, went their way and the owls began to dominate the crepuscular and nocturnal hunting scene. A range of owl species evolved to exploit the various opportunities offered by the developing natural world. From this period we have fossils from the genera *Bubo, Otus, Strix* and *Speotyto*.

From the end of the Miocene period until the present time, palaeontologists think that birds may have enjoyed some sort of heyday, with many more species worldwide than today. Bearing in mind the difficulties in finding fossils, the fact that we know of forty-four species of owl from 500,000 years ago, thirty of which are still extant today, seems to support this view. Perhaps, from the birdwatcher's and photographer's point of view, the most exciting addition to the owls in these relatively modern times is the spectacular Snowy Owl, which probably developed in close association with the series of glaciations of the Miocene period, the ice ages.

But what of owl relatives: from what ancestral stock did owls descend, and which birds are their present-day relatives? Here again, annoyingly, the fossil record lets us down. One simple supposition is that owls and daylight birds of prey came from a single stock. Indeed there are some superficial similarities in beaks, feet and eyes,

This owlet-nightjar, photographed in Australia, is possibly another distant relative of the owl. It is both owl-like and nightjar-like enough to puzzle those naming it, so they took an easy way out.

but these features are in both cases adaptations to a way of life. Such adaptations can easily arise simultaneously in different groups, and are not necessarily indicative of a true relationship. Another theory would link owls to nightjars and similar birds. Although at first sight this may seem likely to be another case of 'parallel evolution' to suit a nocturnal life, new techniques in taxonomy (the naming of species) indicate that the egg-white proteins of the two groups show sufficient similarity to suggest that the relationship may be genuine, and that owls and nightjars (and interestingly also falcons, as distinct from other raptors) may have had a common ancestor in the distant past. We must look forward hopefully to more fossil evidence being uncovered to support or refute this theory. Intriguingly, it could happen any day.

Owls of all sorts and sizes
Museum researchers expert in the taxonomy and classification of owls may not always agree exactly as to how many owls there are. Some would wish to divide obviously closely related birds into two separate species, while others may wish to see the two, perhaps at the lesser rank of subspecies, merged into just a single full species. But these are minor differences of degree, and need not concern us unduly.

Present-day owls are all placed in one taxonomic *order*: the Strigiformes; and this order contains two *families*: the Tytonidae and the Strigidae. The Tytonidae, with only two subfamilies each composed of a single genus, contains the Barn, Grass and Bay Owls; ten species in all. The other family is also divided into two subfamilies,

27

but as it contains all the rest of the owls, is naturally much bigger. The larger of the subfamilies, the Buboninae, or typical owls, contains one hundred species separated into sixteen genera, while the other, the Striginae, or Wood Owls, contains twenty-three species in six genera.

Thus, in all, there are 133 species of owls catalogued in the modern world, but one, the Laughing Owl, *Sceloglaux albifacies*, may be extinct, and one or two others may be teetering on the verge of extinction, not having been seen alive for some years.

Owls come in an astonishing range of sizes, from sparrow to eagle. Further variety is added by the fact that in many owls, as in many birds of prey, the female of the species may be considerably larger than the male, and although this may only amount to a few centimetres in height or wingspan, she may be so much more robust as to be double his weight.

Probably the smallest of the owls is the Elf Owl (*Micrathene*) standing 13 or 14 cm (5 or 5½ ins) high, sparrow-sized and with a wingspan less than the span of a man's hand. Slightly bigger – say starling-sized – are the Pygmy Owlets (*Glaucidium*) at 14-17 cm (5½-6½ ins), the pigeon-sized Little Owl (*Athene*) and the *Otus* group which contains the Screech Owls of the New World and the Scops Owls of the Old. These stand in the 17-25 cm (6½-10 ins) height range.

The middle-sized group of owls – roughly chicken-sized – contains what we might feel to be the 'normal' or 'everyday' owls like the Tawny Owl, which is one of the Wood Owls (*Strix*). Others in this group are the Barn Owls (*Tyto*), familiar almost the world over, the Eared Owls (*Asio*), and the *Ninox* Hawk Owls of the Australasian and Oriental regions and their northern equivalent *Surnia ulula*. Most of these stand between 35 and 45 cm (14-18 ins), with a wingspan of about 1 metre (39 ins), although this varies considerably with the hunting technique, being specially long, for example, in the Short-eared Owl, *Asio flammeus*, which hunts in gliding flight like a harrier and has a very similar wing set-up.

The group of owls of largest size contains some really splendid birds. You could say they were turkey-sized, but eagle-sized sounds grander and more appropriate. At the bottom end of the scale there are the Fishing Owls (*Ketupa* and *Scotopelia*) at 50-60 cm (20-23½ ins), followed by the Snowy Owl (*Nyctea*) at 55-65 cm (21½-25½ ins). The Snowy Owl is relatively long-winged, and looks in the distance more like a slow-flying white egret than an owl. The most stately (if that adjective can be applied to such a ferocious bird) of these large owls are the Eagle Owls (*Bubo*). As their name implies, they are eagle-sized and by far the most powerful of the owls, being able to attack and kill small deer. Eagle Owls vary considerably in size in the various parts of the world, but a big European *Bubo bubo* would stand at 70 cm (27½ ins). The Great Grey Owl (*Strix nebulosa*) may reach 85 cm (33½ ins), considerably taller than an Eagle Owl, but Great Grey Owls live in the forests of the boreal climatic zone close to the Arctic Circle, where temperatures are often very low. As a result, much of the Great Grey Owl's apparent bulk is composed of soft feathers with excellent thermal insulation properties to protect it against this cold. Generally,

Opposite: Their facial discs already well developed, two young Long-eared Owls, out of the nest but still downy and not yet ready to fly, fix the camera both by eye and ear.

Left: *Though not the biggest, the Snowy Owl must be one of the most spectacular of owls. This is a male, slightly smaller than the female and with fewer dark spots.* Right: *The Galapagos Short-eared Owl, one of the most remote races of this widespread bird.*

Great Grey Owls weigh between 1 and 2 kilograms (2.2-4.4 lbs), against a big female Eagle Owl which may weigh up to 4 kilograms (8.8 lbs). Astonishingly, this means the biggest owl species may tip the scales at one hundred times the weight of the smallest!

The range of owl habitats
It is almost fair to say that if you name a habitat, some owl, or several owls, somewhere, will exploit it. The majority of the owl family are birds of forest or woodland, and the glades within this broad habitat category. Owls inhabit woodlands of all sorts, from the cathedral heights of tropical rainforest and the much drier *Acacia* woodlands of the plains of East Africa, through the broad-leaved woodlands typical of temperate regions (like much of Europe) and north, first into pine forest and then to boreal birch woods. Such habitat tends to contain the greatest variety and sometimes the greatest number (or 'biomass' in scientific terms) of potential prey for the owls to exploit. In consequence of this richness and variety of food supply, a range of owls are able to exploit the woodland habitat, from the tiny Pygmy Owls of the genus *Glaucidium* to the giants of the owl world, the Eagle Owls of the genus *Bubo*. Thus, instead of a number of owl species competing for the same food supply, the different diets of the various owls allows the area to be fully exploited without harmful competition.

The margin, where woodland changes into grassland, is often not at all distinct – the thorn-dotted plains so rich in game in Africa are a good example. In Britain, it is possible to conjecture that at the time of the birth of Christ, much of the country was

30

covered in unbroken forest. Since then, and mostly in the last five hundred years, demands for wood (for houses, ships and fuel) and for farmland (to feed our growing population) have whittled away the solid treescape, leaving a patchwork of woods, spinneys, copses and hedges with crops between. This more open farmscape, together with natural open areas like moorland and open grassy plains is the characteristic habitat of the Barn Owl, which in its many geographical races, achieves an almost world-wide distribution. Related species, like the two Grass Owls, as their name suggests, are particularly associated with pure grassy plains. The Short-eared Owl, another species with an enormous range, including even remote oceanic island groups like the Galapagos, exploits the same environment but operates perhaps more by day than by night.

Turning to more specialized habitats, the lakes and rivers of the tropics (and, less often, elsewhere) with well-wooded banks, are exploited by two groups of Fishing Owls – for all the world, to my mind, like nocturnal equivalents of those two splendid daytime fish specialists – the world-wide osprey and the various fishing eagles of Africa and Asia. The Fishing Owls of Asia are in the genus *Ketupa*, and those of Africa in the genus *Scotopelia*, totalling seven species in all. Although it is thought that the two are related way back in time, they do not look at all alike. True, the legs and feet of both are similarly adapted to suit their way of life (p. 69), but the general plumage is vastly different. The various *Ketupa* species are massive in size, and share the horned, ferocious look and glaring orange eyes of the Eagle Owls. One of them, Blakiston's Fish Owl, is remarkable in that it penetrates well north into Siberia, where only a few rivers remain unfrozen all year round. The African Fish Owls are much the same size, but are much looser-feathered and rounder-headed, with all-dark eyes and poorly-marked facial discs, giving them the much more placid appearance of an untidy, badly made but cuddly toy.

The white plumage of that most magnificent of owls, the Snowy Owl, gives us a clear indication that it is a tundra bird, exploiting treeless terrain where snow often remains unthawed year-round. Here, summer is a very brief few weeks of warmth, exploited at feverish pace by the various inhabitants, which range from the midges that descend in ravenous hordes on the photographer, immobilized and of necessity motionless in his hide, to the lemmings that provide much of the Snowy Owls' food (and, incidentally and surprisingly, that of many skuas too). The various Arctic-breeding waterfowl and waders demonstrate that high-speed, long-range migrants are most adept at exploiting brief periods of biological productivity.

Whilst many British people think of the Little Owl as one of 'their own' birds, characteristic of open woodland and farmland with plenty of old gnarled trees like pollard willows around field margins, they should remember that it is only during the last one hundred years that it has become established following its artificial introduction into Britain. Some of the more unusual sites for Little Owl nests in Britain, in crevices in sea cliffs or quarry faces, give us a clue to its rocky and arid natural habitat around the Mediterranean. Here, and eastwards through Asia, the Little Owl is a bird of semi-desert areas, in Arabia often found in genuine desert. The Burrowing Owl of the Americas tells a similar story: it is a bird of open, dry grassland and pampas, often nesting in disued prairie dog or viscacha burrows, and like the grass itself and these two burrowing mammals, penetrating with

31

The camera equipment set up to capture the two preceding photographs. Two Braun flash banks were fired by breaking an infra-red photo-cell circuit. The white cone is a dummy flash head.
Preceding pages: *A Little Owl approaching its nest entrance carrying a vole for its young, and departing to hunt again.*

varying degrees of success the really arid, scantily vegetated areas that we call deserts. Certainly the tiny Elf Owl – one of the two smallest owls – would satisfy the strictest purist, as it commonly nests in holes in the giant saguaro cacti in the deserts of Mexico.

Although it may seem as if there is a specialist owl for every occasion, we should not forget that most owls (like many other birds) are flexible creatures in behaviour and diet, and are opportunist enough to exploit any opening. Perhaps the change from woodland edge to farmland has made relatively little difference – Barn Owls and Little Owls can still find some sorts of mice or beetles – but the conversion of country into town must cause drastic changes. A prime example of success in these circumstances is seen in the Tawny Owl, which from its dense woodland natural habitat has invaded not just the large gardens of suburbia, but also the parks right in our city centres.

Another classic example comes from Vancouver airfield, in British Columbia. Here gulls and waders, seeking safety and roosting on the neatly mown grassland between runways, had been causing a major hazard to air traffic. To reduce the risk the airport management decided to allow the grass to grow tall, a measure carefully calculated, on ecological grounds, to make the grass unsuitable for resting birds, which it did. Sadly, though, the management had reckoned without the versatility of nature. The long grass provided an ideal habitat for small rodents, and the

34

Left: *Introduced artificially into Britain, the Little Owl is more commonly a bird of rocky and arid habitats. This Little Owl was photographed in the deserts of Jordan, where natural perches are scarce and a telegraph pole makes a welcome vantage point.* Right: *A Little Owl, in typically squat pose, glares at the camera. It is carrying a vole in its bill.*

population quickly expanded to vast numbers, attracting a range of predatory birds. Particularly obvious among these and, because of their slow flight, just as hazardous to aircraft as the gulls had been, were Short-eared Owls, which became so numerous that over five hundred were trapped in a three-year period.

Owls the world over

Owls vary greatly in their distribution patterns. Of the grand total of 8500-odd birds in the world, very few come close to being described as cosmopolitan – occurring in almost all regions. The osprey is one of these, and so, pleasingly, is our friend the Barn Owl. Barn Owls are found in Australasia, from southeast Asia to India, in Arabia and over much of Africa, Europe, and North and South America. Over this wide range, with its varied habitats and the opportunities for isolation that occur naturally, the Barn Owl has developed over thirty geographical races, many of them confined to islands (which offer the best isolation of all). Of the other seven *Tyto* species, five occur only in Australasia; three of these are restricted to a few islands but the other two, the Sooty Owl, *T.tenebricosa*, and the Masked Owl, *T.novaehollandiae*, are widely distributed in Australia itself. The remaining two species are the Grass Owls, of which one is restricted to Madagascar and the other, the Common Grass Owl, *T.capensis*, is widespread across Africa, India and south-east Asia. Of the two Bay Owls in the related genus *Phodilus*, the African Bay Owl,

35

P.prigoginei, has been found only in the Congo, while the Common Bay Owl, *P.badius*, is seemingly widespread in southeast Asia, though little studied.

The genus *Otus* contains the Screech and Scops Owls. The Screech Owls are exclusively New World creatures, and fall naturally into two groups. The ten or so species from forest habitats in Central and South America are very restricted in their distributions, with little overlap, but one, the Vermiculated Screech Owl, *O.guatemalae*, occurs in mountain woodlands over much of tropical America. The Screech Owls of open woodland and scrub range widely from Alaska to Argentina. In North America, the Eastern and Western Screech Owls, *O.asio* and *O.kennicotti*, are separated by the Rockies, but both are widespread, as is the Choliba Screech Owl, *O.choliba*, in South America. There are another two species, one restricted to Peru, the other to mangrove swamps on the Pacific coast.

The Scops Owls are the Old World part of this genus. Like the Screech Owls, a number of species have isolated distributions but two are widespread. The Collared Scops, *O.bakkamoena*, of Asia is an open woodland bird, common even in large gardens on city margins and spreading further, as more prime forest is removed for timber or to make way for agriculture. Meanwhile, this type of development is having a detrimental effect on forest species like the Reddish and Spotted Scops Owls, *O.rufescens* and *O.spilocephalus*. The Common Scops Owl, *O.scops* (which contains *O.sunia*, the Oriental Scops, thought by some to be a distinct species), ranges right across southern Europe and North Africa into southeast Asia, and also occurs widely in Africa south of the Sahara in the open savannah woodlands.

At the other end of the size scale are the twelve Eagle Owl species. The Eurasian Eagle Owl, *Bubo bubo*, has, as its name suggests, a wide range across most of Europe to the Pacific coasts of Asia, from Scandinavia and Russia in the north to North Africa and India in the south. As would be expected, there is considerable variety in size and plumage colour over this range, and many subspecies have been proposed. The Great Horned Owl, *B.virginianus*, is the only New World representative of *Bubo*, but has a range just as impressive as its Old World counterpart, from the boreal forests of Canada south to Tierra del Fuego. The other ten Eagle Owls have much more restricted ranges, six in Africa separated by subtle differences in habitat, and four in southeast Asia. One, the Dusky Eagle Owl, *B.coromandus*, inhabits open woodland and riverine forest over a considerable range from India to Malaysia, but the others are restricted in widely separated areas of montane forest.

The Fishing Owls (genus *Ketupa* in Asia, *Scotopelia* in Africa) being so specialized in their feeding are naturally somewhat restricted, but perhaps more in numbers than in range. Three of the Asian species are separated geographically, but the fourth and most widespread Brown Fish Owl, *K.zeylonensis*, ranges from the Middle East to southeast Asia. Presumably some neat ecological distinction prevents undue competition when its range overlaps the others. Indeed the Tawny Fish Owl, *K.flavipes*, seems to give good evidence of this, as it is an upland bird. There

Opposite, above: *A Masked Owl in full threat display – a most impressive sight for so huge a bird. This is a so-called 'dark phase' bird with distinct chestnut tones to its face and breast.* Opposite, below: *The Spix or Choliba Screech Owl takes over the role of the Screech Owl over much of eastern South America in dry woodland and bush country.*

Left: *Superficially similar in size and shape to the New World Screech Owl, the Scops Owl of the Old World is usually much greyer in plumage. At close quarters, the feather markings are unbelievably fine and delicate, and contribute to the excellent camouflage that allows these birds to roost undetected even in city squares.*
Right: *The Eastern Screech Owl is widespread across North America east of the Rockies. It is a woodland bird, its short rounded wings making it one of the most agile and manoeuvrable hunters.*

seems to be more overlap within the three African species, though one, the Rufous Fishing Owl, *S.ussheri*, is extremely rare and another, *S.bouvieri*, the Vermiculated Fishing Owl, we know little about. Of even the most widespread, Pel's Fishing Owl, *S.peli*, which occurs over much of Africa south of the Sahara, we could hardly claim to know much about its habits.

The three owls of the genus *Pulsatrix* – the Spectacled Owls – must be counted by anyone as amongst the most elegant of owls. All come from Central or South America, and two are rare and of local distribution. We know little about even the most widespread, the Spectacled Owl, *P.perspicillata*, save that it is a bird of tropical rain forests in Central America, and that it is fortunately demonstrating its versatility by colonizing secondary forest and even farmland following the clearance of its ancestral habitat.

Some of the five species in the genus *Ciccaba* compete with the Spectacled Owls for elegance, especially the Black-and-White Owl, *C.nigrolineata*, of Central America and the Black-banded Owl, *C.huhula* (lovely name), of the forest and plantations of the Amazon basin. The Mottled Owl, *C.virgata*, is less distinguished-looking, but the most widely distributed of this group with a range extending in forests from Mexico to Argentina. The only non-American species is the African Wood Owl, *C.woodfordii*, widely distributed through Africa south of the Sahara, which is sadly, from the photographer's viewpoint, a rather dull-plumaged bird.

The Arctic tundra north of the tree line and in a circumpolar belt is the habitat of

Left: *One of the monarchs of the bird world – the Great Horned Owl. The American equivalent of the Eagle Owl of Europe, it is similarly huge and ferocious.* Right: *The White-faced Scops Owl, a most elegant little bird from African savannah woodland, often lays its eggs in the disused nests of other birds, such as buffalo weavers, in acacias.*

the Snowy Owl, *Nyctea scandiaca*, almost as powerful a hunter as the Eagle Owls and capable of taking Arctic hares, although its main food is lemmings. The Northern Hawk Owl, *Surnia ulula* (another lovely name), also has this circumpolar belt distribution but further south, from the fringes of the birch scrub into the northern parts of the various boreal forests.

The three species of Little Owls (*Athene*), though closely related, show a neat geographical separation. The 'British' Little Owl, *A.noctua*, is widespread across Europe, its distribution passing north of the Himalayas to reach China. In the Indian sub-continent lowlands it is replaced by the Spotted Little Owl, *A.brama*, which has a similarly catholic choice of habitat. The third species, the Forest Little Owl, *A.blewitti*, prefers moist montane forest and so slots in neatly between the two on the Himalayan foothills.

The Burrowing Owl, though it looks like an *Athene*, is placed in its own genus *Speotyto*, and, interestingly in view of its specialized lifestyle as an almost terrestrial owl, has as a relative one of the earliest of the fossil owls, implying perhaps that its specialization has been of long-lasting benefit. It is widely distributed in the Americas, with no real equivalent in the Old World apart from the *Athene* species, which will often nest in holes in the ground.

The Elf Owl, *Micrathene whitneyi*, although quite numerous, is sadly confined (for most of us keen on seeing or photographing it) to both seaboards of the southern USA and Mexico, but the charming *Aegolius* group are more widespread. The most

39

Although the head is rather too large and rounded for a real *hawk, the long-tailed silhouette, choice of a prominent perch and daytime activity of the Northern Hawk Owl clearly indicate how it got its name.*
Opposite: The Spectacled Owl. Although it is apparently increasing and benefiting from expanding agriculture in Central America, we know little about its biology. But it is extremely photogenic!

northerly, the Tengmalm's or Boreal Owl, *A. funereus*, occurs in a circumpolar belt of coniferous and mixed deciduous woodland including aspen, birch and poplar. The Saw-whet Owl, *A.acadicus*, is widely distributed across the USA and Canada in dense forest. The other two members of this genus have very restricted distributions, one in Central America, the other 'somewhere in South America'. This last, the Buff-fronted Owl, *A.harrisii*, is so beautiful with its yellowish front, black collar and spectacle markings, and white speckled brown back, that we can only hope soon to know more about it. So far it has been seen by only a handful of ornithologists, but it seems so photogenic that any bird photographer would give his eye-teeth to have it in his viewfinder.

There are twelve species of Pygmy Owl, of which the European *Glaucidium passerinum* is the most widespread, occurring in open forest in a belt about 1000 km (625 miles) wide from Germany and Scandinavia to China. It is a difficult bird to spot, and in my experience very shy of emerging into the open in daylight. When you do see it, however, you may be lucky enough to glimpse it flicking its tail, sometimes cocking it like a wren, or wagging it from side to side like a shrike. The American equivalent is the Northern Pygmy Owl, *G.gnoma* (some authorities think that it may be the same species as the European), which is widely distributed in Western North America, or *G.brasilianum* – the Ferruginous Pygmy Owl – which, as its scientific name suggests, occurs in Brazil, and in many other parts of Central and South America living in the mature forests along the many rivers of the area. The Cuban Pygmy Owl, *G.siju*, as its English name implies, is confined to Cuba. The Least Pygmy Owl, *G.minutissimum*, as one might expect is a very tiny bird and may, at 12 cm (4½ ins), be smaller than some Elf Owls. It has a patchy distribution in woodland in Central and South America.

The remaining Old World species of *Glaucidium* are all called Owlets. The Pearl-spotted Owlet, *G.perlatum*, is widespread in the African savannah and bush country, and there are three other African species with much more restricted distributions. The three Asian species seem to keep from conflict by choosing different habitats. The most widespread, the Barred Jungle Owlet, *G.radiatum*, is a bird of open woodland, scrub and agricultural land in India, while the Collared Pygmy Owlet, *G.brodiei*, is very much a bird of mountain forest and the Cuckoo Owlet, *G.cuculoides*, is a bird of sub-tropical evergreen jungles. The last two extend well into southeast Asia.

If Cuba has one of the Pygmy Owls with the most restricted range, then nearby Jamaica can go one better as it has a genus of owl all its own: *Pseudoscops grammicus*, the Jamaican Owl, which is found nowhere else.

The eleven Wood Owls of the genus *Strix* have a world-wide distribution, omitting only Australasia where perhaps the *Ninox* owls dominate the scene. Only one *Strix*, the Great Grey Owl, *S.nebulosa* – a bird of northern forests – occurs in both Old and New Worlds. There are three *Strix* owls in the Americas with relatively restricted and widely separated ranges, but the large Barred Owl, *S.varia*, is found over much of the eastern half of Canada, USA and Central America, occupying open forest in much the same way as the Ural Owl, *S.uralensis*, does in its broad Old World distribution across north and central Europe and Asia. The Tawny Owl, *S.aluco*, has a wider distribution from north to south, penetrating into north Africa, but does not extend so widely into Asiatic Russia as the Ural Owl.

Of the remaining four, Hume's Wood Owl, *S.butleri*, has a very, restricted distribution in the Near East: it may conceivably be just a desert race of the Tawny Owl, but for a desert-edge bird 'wood owl' is an odd name. The Brown Wood Owl, *S.leptogrammica*, is a forest owl of southeast Asia, while the Mottled Wood Owl, *S.ocellata*, although with a similar if slightly smaller range, is a bird much more of agricultural areas. The Spotted Wood Owl, *S.seloputo*, is relatively common but restricted to the Malaysian lowlands.

The Eared Owls of the genus *Asio* form a compact group with clearly defined distribution patterns. The Long-eared Owl, *A.otus*, is an open forest bird (both deciduous and coniferous) occurring in a broad belt through temperate and north temperate Europe, Asia and North America. There is a very similar species nicely named as the Stygian Owl, *A.stygius*, in the dark forests of South America, and another, again similar, restricted to Madagascar. The Short-eared Owl so familiar

Opposite: *The Cuckoo Owlet (or Barred Pygmy Owl) from southeast Asia is one of the larger members of its group at 25 cm (10 ins). It is a daylight hunter and quick on the wing, hunting birds in the manner of a sparrowhawk. Viewed from behind (although with typical owl neck flexibility it is keeping the camera clearly in view) the Cuckoo Owlet looks remarkably hawk like – and indeed quite like a young cuckoo so far as plumage is concerned.*

The Boobook Owl, a nocturnal hunter, feeding largely on insects. 'Boobook' is a human transliteration of the distinctive call of this most widespread of Australasian owls.
Opposite, above: Caught by surprise by my flash (the eye pupils are still widely dilated for night vision) a Long-eared Owl peers in annoyance, first from one side of the trunk and then from the other.
Opposite, below: A Short-eared Owl on the ground, showing well the rather 'horizontal' way it holds its body (for easy walking) and the large yellow irises and small pupils of a bird with good daylight vision.

over marsh and moor has a wide distribution in both hemispheres, and although absent from Africa and Australia, it occurs on many remote islands. In Africa, its place is taken by the African Marsh Owl, *A.capensis*, which uses open grasslands and marshes south of the Sahara for hunting.

The last group to be discussed here are the *Ninox* owls. These seem to be relatively primitive, and the recent fossil record would suggest perhaps that they have been displaced by more up-to-date species over much of the world. However, like those primitive marsupials the kangaroos, the *Ninox* owls have found a last refuge in Australasia, where sufficient isolation has allowed these relics of the past to persist undisturbed, and to occupy a wide range of habitats in the absence of competitors. The Boobook Owl, *N.novaeseelandiae*, is perhaps the most widely distributed right across Australia and New Zealand in a wide variety of habitats, rather like the Tawny Owl. It is replaced further to the north and through southeast Asia by the Oriental Hawk Owl, *N.scutulata*, with similarly catholic habitat preferences. Most

45

of the other *Ninox* owls have a much more restricted distribution, often to just an island or two, but three others: *N.connivens*, the Barking Owl (a bird of more open bush country); *N.rufa*, the Rufous Owl (dense riverine woodland); and *N.strenua*, the Powerful Owl (montane forest and the Australian equivalent of the Ural Owl) manage to coexist peacefully in Australia with the Boobook.

Sources of knowledge of owls

Considering the popularity of owls, it is surprising that we know so little about them. True, they have a wide range of specialized adaptations, but in many ways they lend themselves to detailed study, for example by producing convenient pellets (see p. 73) which allow detailed analyses of variations in their diet. Perhaps the root of the problem lies in the fact that owls function best when we function worst, after dark. Moreover, most birdwatchers are situated in Europe and North America, where the number of owl species is small. Elsewhere in the world, our knowledge of the owl family is scanty, to say the least. In some cases, the sheer difficulty of just reaching and penetrating the remote terrain where owls have their territories has been sufficient to preclude detailed study. The African Bay Owl 'survives' as a handful of museum specimens, and the Long-whiskered Owlet from Peru (which appeared in a net to surprise and delight its captors, a group of American ornithologists) has only been known to *exist* for a few years.

Despite these problems, determined enthusiasts over the years have accumulated considerable information on many owl species, and those of us interested in learning much more about these fascinating birds are greatly in their debt. Much of their work is published in scientific journals that may not be easy to locate, but fortunately, in the last decade or so, several books have been compiled drawing together this knowledge. The following are recommended:

BENT, A. C., *Life Histories of North American Birds of Prey*, Dover Publications Inc, New York, 1958.
BROWN, L. H., *African Birds of Prey*, Collins, London 1970.
BURTON, JOHN A. (Ed), *Owls of the World: Their Evolution, Structure and Ecology*, Peter Lowe, London, 1973.
EVERETT, M., *A Natural History of Owls*, Hamlyn, London, 1977.
GEROUDET, P., *Les Rapaces Diurnes et Nocturnes d'Europe*, Pelachaux et Niestle, Neuchâtel, 1965.
GROSSMAN, M. L. and HAMLET, J., *Birds of Prey in the World*, Clarkson N. Potter Inc, New York, 1964.
SPARKS, J. and SOPER, T., *Owls: Their Natural and Unnatural History*, David and Charles, Devon; Taplinger, New York, 1970.

For those wishing to know more about the identification of owls in the field in various parts of the world, there are now illustrated, more or less pocket-sized, field guides available for many regions. These are now so many in number that to list them all would be impractical, but a good bird bookshop should easily be able to supply appropriate details.

Opposite: *Browner to suit its habitat, the African Marsh Owl in many ways resembles the Short-eared Owl, preferring open country. Perhaps because it feeds largely on insects, it is mainly nocturnal – a marked contrast to the Short-eared Owl.*

A Way of Life

Dressed to kill

All owls are effective hunters. Some operate largely during daylight hours, skilfully locating their quarry and catching it by surprise. Whilst birds of prey like eagles, hawks and falcons are perhaps supreme daylight hunters, it is those owls which hunt in fading evening light, during darkness, or even in the utter blackness of a moonless night, that are the most sophisticated of all the hunters of the natural world. Let us see what 'weapon systems' evolution has designed for them to achieve this success.

After the normal functions such as insulation and providing the mechanism for flight, first and foremost the feathers of owls have become adapted to silence their flight. This has two clear benefits. First, that the prey that is being stalked by an owl in flight, or watched by one on a lookout perch, cannot hear the hushed approach of the hunter. Second, the owl is very often dependent on its own ears to detect the slightest sound made by its potential meal: the quieter its own feathers as it flies, or adjusts its position on a perch, the easier it can detect prey.

A close inspection of (say) a Tawny Owl wing illustrates the techniques. Viewed from the underside, the body and wing feathers of a Tawny Owl look just like those of any other bird – a central shaft with rows of neatly-ordered barbs on each side, all hooked together by microscopic barbules in the system that make feathers flexible but strong. The surface of the chitin of which the feathers are made seems reasonably hard and slightly shiny. Reverse the feather, and what a difference you see. In velvet or corduroy cloth, the reverse of the fabric is a tough and workmanlike crossweave, while the face is soft to the touch, its pile of many small threads providing a lightweight but warm cloth. Remember how silently velvet fabrics swing? The principle of owl feathers is much the same. The upper surface of each feather is covered in a myriad soft short filaments, giving it precisely the appearance and feel of velvet and greatly silencing its passage through the air.

But owls have other tricks up their sleeves. In most birds, the leading edge of the wing is relatively inflexible and hard to the touch. As it moves, it makes a distinct 'swish' – just as you would get from sweeping a wooden ruler sharply through the air. In many owls, the leading-edge barbs are of varied length, and are clustered in groups to form a serrated or comb-like fringe. This so breaks up the air flow over the

Opposite: *Every muscle straining at the end of the power stroke down-beat, a Little Owl leaves its nest.*

49

Left: *A Little Owl springs off from its nest hole.* Right: *The hunched back and determined expression indicate the power that the Little Owl puts into its downstroke.*

wing edge that it assists most effectively in silencing the flight.

Over and above this, most owls, because of their unusually fluffy plumage, appear much bigger than they actually are. Their wings, though, are long or broad or both. So the body-weight load placed on the wings is relatively low compared with other birds, and allows slower (and thus quieter) wingbeats and spells of quite silent gliding.

This seems a sensible point to mention some of the secondary features of owl plumage. Straightforward insulation from the cold has already been referred to, and is particularly important in those species inhabiting nothern forests, taiga or tundra and those on high mountain ranges. Strange as it may seem, despite the heat of the day, deserts can be very cold at night, so even the desert fringe owls do need protection.

Many birds have 'cryptic' patterns on their feathers: patterns which help conceal them from predators. The great majority of female birds, which of necessity sit on nests for long periods, benefit from the camouflage of streaky brown plumages of one sort or another. You might think that owls have no need for camouflage, but the hunter, too, can benefit from dark, drab coloration when on the wing in near-darkness.

Although the Barn Owl in its pale-breasted form is a striking exception to this rule, no explanation can readily be found for this. The other white owl – the Snowy Owl – is of course no exception, as it hunts for much of the time in daylight against a snow-covered background. Camouflage has added benefits for the nocturnal hunters. These must roost during the hours of daylight, and if no convenient hole is available or if they are one of the many species that do not roost in holes anyway, then their camouflage offers some protection from disturbance by aggravating mobbing hordes of alarmed small birds.

Opposite, below: *Rounded wings give the Little Owl the necessary manoeuvrability as it enters its nest. The Little Owl is just one of many owl species round the world that exploit man-made nest sites.*

Left: *Little Owl – the upstroke, finger-tipped wings splayed to allow air to pass through.* Right: *Banking, using the extreme flexibility of its 'variable geometry' wings.*

The tiny Ferruginous Pygmy Owl rarely stands more than 13.5 cm (5½ ins) tall. Despite its small size, the talons are conspicuously large as befits a daytime hunter. Top: Perched and ever on the lookout for a passing bird or rodent. Above: From the back this bird appears to have eyes in the back of its head – an example of the amazing cryptic plumage patterns found in the bird world.

Top: To keep predators at bay this Owl Butterfly (shown upside-down) has its own brand of camouflage in the form of an owl's face in the wing pattern. Above: You can almost feel the velvety surface of this Long-eared Owl wing — excellent for silencing flight.

53

Top, left and right: *The Verreaux's or Milky Eagle Owl is typically a bird of the open woodlands of East Africa. Their colouring and choice of roosting site make these two birds difficult to spot.* Above: *A Boobook Owl – well camouflaged as it roosts in a eucalyptus.*

Generally, camouflage plumages are a delicate mixture of shades of fawn, grey, brown and chestnut, with streaks of black and white. Some owls are very confident in the protection offered, especially the Screech and Scops Owls and the Long-eared Owls, which habitually roost in trees or bushes. When undisturbed, they will perch comfortably loose-feathered and contentedly plump – for all the world like Tawny Owls – quite at ease. Should anything alert them, they quickly clamp down their body feathers, stretching tall at the same time. Astonishingly as it may seem, even when roosting in something as flimsy as a hawthorn bush in winter, in this

Left: *A still photograph cannot convey the characteristic bouncing flight of the Short-eared Owl, but it does show the length of wing and streamlined body.* Right: *Huge against the sky, an Eagle Owl scoops great wingfuls of air as it leaves its nesting gully.*

'vertical format', motionless and with their flecked plumage closely resembling the bark, they look so like a broken-off branch that you may pass by within a few feet unknowing. Should you come accidentally just a bit *too* close, they will slip silently off their perches and swoop away through the trees. Several times I have had the fright of my life at the suddenness of it!

Hunting techniques

Were we to have a comprehensive knowledge of the ecology of all the world's owls, it seems likely that the best general term that we could use to describe their hunting might be 'flexibly opportunist'. True, there are some highly specialized owls (leave aside the overall adaptation to nocturnal hunting) but most can turn their talents to a variety of hunting skills.

There are two broad categories, into which many of the owls fit, with the attractively meaningful colloquial headings of 'perch and pounce' and 'glide and grab'. Into the first category fall many of the short, round-winged owls like the familiar Tawny and Little Owls. Their technique is to choose a good vantage point, with unimpeded lines of sight *and hearing*, and wait more or less motionless for prey to come within range. Then comes the swoop. Sometimes this may be a vertical plummet, with wings held arched like an umbrella to serve as a parachute and control the fall. Other times the owl may fly some distance before finally pouncing. The Northern Hawk Owl also chooses perches in the open, often atop a conifer, and with its long tail and pointed wings, does indeed resemble a heavy-headed hawk. In this Hawk Owl's habitat – the northern fringe of the forest belt and the edges of the tundra – there is almost perpetual daylight during the summer. Although well adapted to hunt by sight in these conditions, the Northern Hawk Owl retains a perfect capability to hunt at night – indeed it has to, for during the winter

Little Owl – in level flight.

daylengths are very short. Despite its hawk-like appearance, most of its food is rodents rather than birds.

Into the 'glide and grab' group fit the owls with relatively long and slender wings, the best known being the Barn Owl, the Long-eared Owl and above all, the Short-eared Owl. Bouncing along in its peculiar but highly characteristic flight, the Short-eared Owl must be familiar to most birdwatchers. Once over its hunting grounds, be they marshes, heather moors, upland rough grazing grassland, or open heath-land, the bouncing flight is interspersed with long silent glides as the owl sweeps low looking for prey. If some unsuspecting small mammal or bird is sighted, the owl banks and turns steeply, plunges, and snatches its prey before the victim has had time to collect its wits. The element of surprise is an important essential in this technique.

Thus a quick glance at the flight silhouette of an owl may often tell us much about how it hunts. In aircraft design terms, it is the 'aspect ratio' (the length/breadth ratio) that gives the clues, and this holds true for many birds. Long wings tend to give flight speed and efficiency for long-range purposes, while short, broad ones give lower speed, lower efficiency but much greater manoeuvrability. So the long, narrow-winged owls are the flying hunters, and the short, round-winged birds are those that sit patiently and wait. Between the two extremes are the more general-

Top: *Long-winged, a Barn Owl leaves its nesting barn. The soft feathers of the upper side of the wing are rising, indicating a strong updraught and giving an indication of the power of lift generated by the aerofoil section of the inboard part of the wing.* Above: *Long in the wing, long in the leg. A Short-eared Owl approaching its nest showing the typical features of a gliding hunter.*

Almost like Concorde coming in to land, a Barn Owl, elegance personified, approaches the nest with a long-tailed fieldmouse.
Opposite, above: Fiery orange eyes, ferocious expression, all feathers fluffed out in fury and hissing spitefully, few birds of any sort could match an Eagle Owl in aggressive display. Opposite, below: A portrait of the Turkestan Eagle Owl – on this occasion with a reasonably benign expression – showing in detail the beauty of the eye pigmentation and the complex but delicate structure of the facial disc feathers. In poor light the pupil will expand until almost no orange iris shows.

purpose owls, mixing their hunting techniques, and their diets, as opportunity allows.

Sensory systems

Owls' eyes are often startlingly lemon-yellow or fiery in iris coloration, and even when as liquid-brown as those of the Tawny Owl, are always large. They are surrounded by a facial disc of feathers which are often strikingly patterned, and this seems to enhance the prominence – and thus the practical importance – of the eyes. It is easy to think that owls rely on these large eyes to overcome the difficulties of hunting in darkness, but this is only partly true, as many owls also have extremely highly developed hearing. Let us look at the eyes first.

Top: *The hawk-like head of the Powerful Owl of Australia. Probably rather primitive, these owls have very poorly developed facial discs.* Above: *A Great Horned Owl, head thrown back in a dramatic display.*

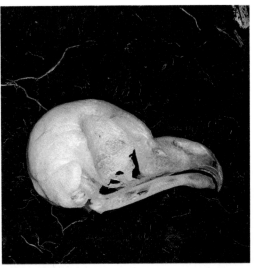

Left: *Slightly mournful in appearance, and not a little untidy, this Tawny Owl is closing its 'third eyelid' or nictitating membrane, which moves across the eye to clean it and to protect it.* Right: *The skull of a Tawny Owl. So sophisticated are the sensory systems that, of the roughly spherical part behind the beak, almost half is taken up by the eye sockets, and a considerable part of the remainder houses the hearing apparatus.*

The eyes of owls face straight forwards, as do our own. This is a characteristic of the hunter, rather than the hunted. Just as lions have eyes facing forwards, and their antelope prey have eyes facing largely sideways, so owls (and the other birds of prey) have eyes facing forwards, while their prey (be it birds or rodents) have eyes facing sideways. The reasons are highly practical: the fields of view of the two forward-facing eyes overlap to some extent, and produce what is called 'binocular vision'. This enhances the stereoscopic effect of what we see, but also allows very precise judgement of distances – just as the two lenses of the rangefinders on my old Leicas used to do. Such judgement is clearly important for a hunter, and perhaps vital to one on the wing. Man and the apes possess binocular vision not so much for hunting but more for manual dexterity. Fine judgement of distance is also necessary for the manipulatory skills that evolution has endowed us with.

The hunted, of course, have similarly good reasons for having their eyes placed laterally. Judgement of distance for them is of relatively little importance. Far more practical and valuable is as wide a field of view as possible, so that approaching predators may be quickly detected. In some animals, and in birds like the stone curlew and woodcock, the eyes are so placed as to give the maximum 360° of all-round vision.

The eyes of owls are relatively much larger than those of other birds, and they occupy most of the 'face' of the owl's skull. So large are they, and so oddly shaped (rather like a jeweller's eye-glass) that they have very limited movement within their sockets – far less than our own. To compensate for this, owls have evolved very special necks, which allow their heads to rotate through at least 180° (they can look straight behind them) and sometimes almost right 'round the clock' to 300° or more! A special configuration of the jugular veins, with linked by-pass blood ves-

61

As a 'perch and pounce' hunter, the Little Owl needs a flexible neck to keep an eye on potential prey with the minimum of movement to betray its presence.

sels, ensures that the blood supply to and from the brain is not impeded.

Like other birds the owl possesses a nictitating eyelid – a thin membrane which passes across the eyes to wash them and keep them free from dust and dirt. Interestingly, in the owl's case this membrane is opaque whereas with most other birds it is transparent.

Just how good are owls at seeing in the dark? The answer must depend on the interpretation of 'dark', as owls (and other creatures) cannot 'see' in *total* darkness. But then total darkness rarely, if ever, occurs naturally, as outdoors there is always some (albeit very little) light. This is when owls excel. The very size of their eyes, and particularly the size of the wide-opened pupil (often far larger than in humans) is a clear indication that the eye is well designed to gather what light there is, and a powerful lens concentrates this light on the sensitive retina placed close behind it.

Within the retina there are two types of light-sensitive receptor cells, 'rods' and 'cones', named roughly after the shape of the cells. Most daylight creatures have a preponderance of cones, which function best at high light intensities and allow accurate perception of detail and colour. Such cells are particularly numerous and

A Little Owl, standing tall in part of its bobbing display designed to intimidate intruders.

well developed in high-flying birds like vultures and eagles, allowing them to spot prey thousands of feet below. Cones work very badly in poor light. At the other end of the scale are the rods, which function best at low light levels, and although not producing an image of such clarity or detail as the cones, allow the owls (which have a particularly high proportion of rods in the retina) to see very effectively in conditions that would incapacitate most other animals.

It is often said that this high ability to see in the dark results in near-blindness during daylight hours for the owl, but this is not so. Some owls actually hunt most in daylight – the Short-eared Owl, for example. Others, like the Barn and Little Owls frequently hunt in daylight, and quite effectively. A resting owl will naturally close its eyes – and most owls rest through the day – hence the 'screwed up' facial expression in bright light. The pupils, too, are bound to be small in the light as the eye is so light-sensitive. Maybe the owls' daylight vision is not quite so good as some other birds, but demonstrably it is perfectly adequate.

Now the ears. Let me at once dispel any idea that the conspicuous tufts of feathers sprouting from the sides of the head, roughly where you would expect ears to be,

The finely vermiculated plumage of the Collared Scops Owl gives excellent camouflage against rocks or tree trunks.
Opposite: *This Long-eared Owl, staring fixedly at the camera, is also using its facial disc as a reflector to concentrate the slightest of sounds onto its ears. Notice the nictitating eyelids.*

64

Left: *A portrait of the Spectacled Owl: surely one of the neatest and most distinctive facial disc patterns.*
Right: *The downy feathers on the throat of the Pharaoh Eagle Owl puff out when the bird hoots.*

are anything to do with hearing. They are not – and do not let names like Long-eared and Short-eared Owls confuse you. The precise function of these tufts is unknown; they are probably used during display, as are other parts of the plumage.

The ears themselves, though superficially invisible, are far more exciting organs, and in owls are perhaps at the peak of development in the animal kingdom. They are fantastically sophisticated, and of great importance as a parallel sensory system to the eyes in poor light conditions. If ever you come across the corpse of an owl killed on the road, lift up the feathers on the side of the head. Beneath the slightly rigid 'flap' of feathers that you have lifted, on each side is an enormous crescentic ear-hole. You will notice that the two ears are not symmetrically placed on either side of the head, nor are they usually the same size and shape.

The reason for the size is fairly obvious – all the better to hear with. The reason for the lack of symmetry is intensely practical, and another example of high-technology evolution. During the early days of the last war, before radar was widely used, approaching enemy aircraft were detected by audio range-finders. These basically resembled two gigantic ear trumpets, and to obtain maximum accuracy in judging an aircraft s distance, it was soon found that the tubes connecting the trumpets to the listener's ears were best of unequal length. The owls had worked this one out several million years earlier!

In some owls, the relatively hard bristly feathers of the facial disc are thought to serve as reflectors – in the same way that a sound recordist would use a parabolic reflector to focus bird song into the microphone of his tape recorder. Good evidence for this comes from the Long-eared Owl. When roosting during the day, not only are the eyes tight shut but the whole face seems crumpled. Should a sudden noise disturb the owl, the feathers are quickly fanned and expanded to form the normal

66

Left: *Neatly clad in cinnamon, brown and white, a Spotted Wood Owl.* Right: *An immature Spotted Eagle Owl glares at the camera.*

face disc, and the head turns slowly to locate the sound and identify it. The facial disc might appear to compensate for the lack of 'ears' or pinnas, the flaps of skin supported by cartilage, that we humans and many other mammals use to gather sound and channel it to our eardrums. But in fact the owl ear, beneath the feathers, is surrounded by a very mobile flap of skin that can be adjusted by small muscles to concentrate sound from any direction.

Fascinating experiments with several species of owls have shown them able, with almost unerring accuracy, to locate by sound and strike their prey in the total darkness of a large light-proof room. Long-eared and Great Horned Owls are amongst those to have demonstrated this ability most dramatically. With such acute sight and hearing, so well developed that the visual and audio organs seem to fill the skull, mounted on a head so effective that it resembles nothing so much as a miniature radar scanner, it is no wonder that owls are so successful after dark.

The tools of the trade

Most owls have relatively short legs – perhaps what you would expect from their rather squat, upright posture. There are exceptions, though, apparently mostly associated with adaptations to suit a particular and rather specialist mode of life. The most familiar of these exceptions is the Barn Owl. A quick thought about its 'upside-down pear' stance gives the idea that it is long legged, and this is confirmed on close inspection as the legs are often clearly visible. If you are lucky enough ever to handle a Barn Owl – a road casualty perhaps – then the length of leg is positively striking.

If a Barn Owl's flight and hunting techniques remind us of the harrier's, then it is perhaps not so surprising that evolution has endowed the Barn Owl with extra-

long legs, just as in the harriers. As in harriers, too, the legs are often carried dangling down, claws clenched, in flight. For a bird gliding across mixed, but normally quite short, cover and suddenly dropping to seize prey, these long legs are an asset as they allow a snatch to be made without the plumage or especially the wings getting caught up on the vegetation.

Much the same can be said of the Fishing Owls. Most are little-studied, but we do know that they hunt like an osprey or one of the fish eagles, swooping down and snatching a basking fish from just beneath the water surface. Not only are the Fishing Owls' legs long, but as a further adaptation the tarsus (or 'shin', though that is not its correct name) is unfeathered, quite unlike the other owls. This must save them a lot of drying and preening time. The exception seems to be Blakiston's Fish Owl, from the Far East, which is shorter in the leg and has feathered tarsi. We know little about its ecology, but it does spend much time wading about in the shallows seeking out crayfish to eat.

The feet of Fishing Owls serve as an excellent example of parallel evolution as well as of adaptation to a specialized ecology. As I said, the legs and feet are unfeathered, and the talons are typically long and sharp. The undersides of the toes are covered in tough, rough pimply skin. This gives a grip – needed for such very slippery prey. The soles of the feet look, feel and function very like the feet of those other unrelated bird fishing specialists, the osprey and the African fish eagle.

The feet of the Snowy Owl show almost the reverse adaptation. As birds of low-temperature areas, they need good body insulation, which their light fluffy feathers admirably provide. But they also spend much of the time perched on convenient viewpoints like hummocks or boulders, and in the snow and perma-frost of their normal habitat, could quickly lose dangerous amounts of body warmth through their feet, or suffer frost-bite. To counter this, they have evolved densely feathered feet and toes, extremely attractive as well as highly effective. They remind me greatly of the feet of the ptarmigan, a mountaintop game bird adapted to endure similarly harsh conditions.

In the owls, as in all the other birds of prey (save vultures which, as carrion feeders, do not need powerful feet) the feet are the vital weapon in catching and killing the prey. It is very interesting to see the parallels here between the various groups. The theme is always the same: the toes are long and strong, powered by robust muscles and tendons, and set 'four-square', with almost a right-angle between each. Unlike in many smaller birds, and in ducks and waders where it may be reduced almost to nothing, the fourth or hind toe is little smaller than the other three. A typical approach, just before striking the prey (whether that prey is on the wing, on a branch, or on the ground), would be with legs slightly apart and outstretched and toes splayed wide to give the maximum possible catching area.

The toes are tipped with unusually long, strong and very sharp claws: they react instantly on contact, and often penetrate the prey causing mortal damage almost immediately. Otherwise the life may be literally squeezed from the luckless victim,

Opposite: *Feather maintenance is vitally important to all birds, owls included. The body and wing feathers can be passed through the beak, but of course the head feathers are out of reach, except to a dexterously used claw – as this Tawny Owl demonstrates.*

69

Top: *The feather-clad talons of the male Snowy Owl – an adaptation to insulate the feet from snow or frozen soil.* Above, left: *A good illustration of the huge span of the toes and the length and sharpness of the talons in the Pharaoh Eagle Owl.* Above, right: *Clearly well suited to a life of running about on the ground, nesting in a subterranean burrow, these legs belong to the Burrowing Owl.*

or if it struggles in a troublesome (and potentially dangerous) way like the snakes that the Great Horned Owl is fond of catching, then the *coup de grâce* may be administered by a powerful bite into the neck behind the head.

The massive feet and talons of the larger owls – especially the Eagle Owls – seem fearsome weapons to have to counter even in human terms, but the owl beak, although it is large, hooked and typically hawk-like, is only rarely used in aggression except at the kill. More often, the beak is used to manipulate prey, or dismember it for feeding to owlets.

Food and feeding

In common with all other birds, owls have no teeth. This means that they must either swallow their prey whole, or tear it into suitably-sized chunks, usually

Top: This male Snowy Owl is barking a warning. Much as the beak may appear small, the mouth can open very wide – ideal if much of the prey is swallowed whole. Above: Owl castings, or pellets, composed of the indigestible remains of meals. From the left: Little, Long-eared, Short-eared, Tawny and Barn Owl.

dismembering it by removing the head or limbs. Most prey items, though, are swallowed whole, a process greatly assisted by the very large gape. Although most of the jaws are hidden beneath the feathers, the mouth is quite snake-like and wide, opening almost literally from ear to ear so that large prey can be swallowed. Once the prey is in the gullet, however, the swallowing process may slow down slightly through sheer lack of space, and I have often been amused in my hide to see the tail of a rodent protruding slightly from the beak of a well-grown nestling. It may take some hours of struggling before it finally vanishes!

An owl's digestive system is obviously pretty powerful, and quickly extracts the goodness from the fleshy parts. Small indigestible items like the bristles (chaetae) of eathworms quickly pass through the gut and are excreted, but larger items, ranging from the wing cases (elytra) of beetles through to the fur, feathers and bones of

71

Above, left: *The earthworm will make a substantial meal for this Little Owl's chicks, but many larger owls do not scorn such relatively small meals either.* Above, right: *A Little Owl with a grub for its young. This owl is braking to land, feet outstretched and legs bent to absorb the shock.* Below, left: *A Little Owl on a characteristic perch, with a ground beetle (a common food item) in its beak.* Below, right: *An underground Little Owl nest in a disused rabbit burrow. The prey is a yellow underwing moth.*

Left: *Little Owl approaching its nest hole with a long-tailed fieldmouse firmly grasped in its beak.* Right: *The aerial equivalent of 'backing water' as the Little Owl slows before landing, a cranefly in its beak.*

larger prey, are formed into castings called pellets which the owl expels by regurgitation. Although we tend to think of these dark grey-brown pellets as typical of owls, many other birds which eat insects, shellfish or fish do regularly or occasionally produce them – waders and gulls are good examples.

Pellets offer a valuable guide to what an owl has been eating, and many studies of owl diets are based on pellet analyses. With owls this is particularly convenient, as so many of them are nocturnal hunters and thus not easily observed feeding. Pellets do not provide a complete food record because of the unknown proportion of smaller items that have been destroyed during digestion or which have passed right through the gut, but despite this they offer the opportunity of far more precise studies than are possible for most other groups of birds.

Pellets have an additional fascination because the ordinary birdwatcher can find them: usually there are many near the nest site and often heaps (literally) beneath favourite roosting places. Although hard in appearance, pellets soften quickly in water and are easily dissected. The fragments of skulls and skeletons can be removed with tweezers and cleaned with a needle and fine brush before drying, ready for identification. Over a period of time it is possible to observe changes of diet through the seasons, or to compare the spectrum or prey chosen by the same species of owl in different habitats. In this way the picture soon becomes comprehensive.

73

Top: A hide on a timber scaffold alongside an old Welsh barn containing the nest of the Little Owl pictured below. Above: The Little Owl brings a cockchafer beetle to an eager youngster emerging from the depths of the nest.

Left: *Sometimes food is not far from home – this Barn Owl is both watching and listening intently for signs of movement on the barn floor.* Right: *The short tail indicates that the Barn Owl has caught a vole. Those claws can quickly kill any small rodent they grasp.*

Pellets from woodland Tawny Owls usually contain almost exclusively the remains of small rodents, while those from urban Tawny Owls contain many more remnants of birds. Thus a study of diet through pellets endorses what we have already seen of owl versatility. Probably the majority of owls are opportunists, making the most of what they can easily catch, and well able to 'make do' with such apparently trivial items as worms when their main foods are in short supply. Even a specialist like a Fishing Owl will take rodents or birds if it has the chance, while amphibians and reptiles often feature in the pellets of owls that we would not expect to hunt near water. Some owls, especially the Great Horned Owl, will tackle snakes, their dense soft plumage protecting them well from bites.

Perhaps more surprise stems from the number of owls, particularly in the tropics, that have insects as their major prey. A concentration on large beetles might be expected of the Burrowing Owl with its largely pedestrian terrestrial habits, but the Elf Owl and the Pygmy Owl both catch many large insects on the wing. The Boobook Owl of Australasia, smallest of the *Ninox* owls, feeds mainly on insects, but even stranger, the Akun Eagle Owl, *Bubo leucostictus*, of tropical African forests is reputed to be predominantly an insect-eater, despite its size and appearance. Of the smaller owls, the Cuckoo Owlet is said to be sufficiently swift and agile on the wing to catch not only insects but also a considerable variety of fast-flying birds.

Another surprise is the incidence of 'cannibalism' among predators: clearly there is no honour among thieves. Owls are known to be hunted and caught by larger

75

A very wet Barn Owl. Although owls normally do not hunt in the rain, this one had five youngsters to feed.
Opposite: *A Pearl-spotted Owlet from southern Africa clutching a weaver bird.*

daytime predators – particularly hawks – but they also feature regularly in the pellets of owl species larger than themselves!

Despite the small size of the Akun Eagle Owl prey, other Eagle Owls will take hares and occasionally small deer or antelopes, and we tend to regard them as the most powerful owl hunters. In one sense this is so, but if we compare the weight or the size of the prey with that of the owl, then several other owls turn out to be just as powerful, or more so, size for size. The Little Owl, for example, has been recorded as tackling and killing birds as big as mistle thrushes, jays and jackdaws, while the tiny Pygmy Owl will take on various thrushes and rats sometimes larger than itself!

77

The Breeding Season

When it comes to building a nest – in the sense of a carefully woven construction securely lodged in position in a tree-fork – owls must be at the very bottom of the league table. They make no nest as such at all, but simply lay their eggs on the floor or base of their chosen nest site. Admittedly, there is often a goodly layer of pellets to cushion the eggs, but these are not deliberately accumulated into an actual nest. That said, owls the world over exhibit as much flexibility and opportunism in the selection of nest sites as they do in their choice of food.

Some owls show obvious preferences, but others, like the owls of northern boreal forests, have little choice because they are unlikely to find many man-made structures to commandeer, or because, in the case of the Snowy Owl and its arctic tundra habitat, there are no trees to nest in even if it so wished. There are even some specializations: the Burrowing Owl, terrestrial in habit, chooses holes made by rodents, and the Elf Owl is partial to old woodpecker holes in giant cacti. Otherwise, the range of nest sites varies from below ground, in natural or animal-made cavities, through the ground surface, to beneath brushwood, in natural cavities in trees or cliffs, or in little-used buildings, through to the old nests of a huge variety of other birds. These may be at any height above ground: the main feature seems to be that they need to be fairly substantial structures.

Once on the nest, that same cryptic plumage, with its flecks and speckles of various colours, that conceals the roosting owl so well by day will also conceal the sitting female, even on a small nest, astonishingly well.

The eggs
Owls' eggs, too, seem rather primitive and in keeping with their antiquity amongst birds. They resemble the eggs of some of the reptiles from which birds are descended, being much more spherical than most birds' eggs, rather crumbly and chalky as to shell, and lacking any form of pigmentation. As so many of the chosen nest sites are secluded, and often very dark indeed, this supposedly primitive

Opposite: A possessive Long-eared Owl shuffling down to incubate her eggs. The nest was probably built by a crow in the previous year.
Overleaf: A Short-eared Owl leaps into the air from a typical nest site in rough open grassland, giving an excellent demonstration of the unusual length of her legs. The egg in mid-air testifies how well the owl encloses the clutch of eggs with her body feathers while she is brooding. This one got carried aloft – but survived the short fall.

79

Top: *Barn Owl eggs in a museum collection. Note the considerable size difference between Rhodesia (now Zimbabwe) and the Sudan. The mottling on the Sudanese eggs is staining from the nest surroundings.*
Above: Eggs of Elf Owl (right), Verreaux's Eagle Owl (centre) and Barn Owl (left).

82

feature may have high evolutionary value. In their cavities, or old nests, the eggs are unlikely to roll away, so their roundness is no problem. Thus concealed, they do not need complex colour patterns for camouflage, and in the darkness, white eggs will have a positive value as the female will find them much easier to locate, and they will thus be much safer from accidental damage should she tread on one with a lethal talon.

At the nest
In those owls whose breeding-season biology is well enough known, it seems almost always to be the male who does the displaying, by flight and call, round his chosen territory. This display will first attract and then retain a mate, and in time a firm pair bond will be established. Most owls, so far as we know, are monogamous, but the Snowy Owl is an exception where the male may support two females.

Within the territorial boundaries, there are usually more than enough potential nest sites, be they holes in trees, old crows' nests, or gopher holes. The male owl, and perhaps the female too, will be familiar with most of these and will have roosted in particularly suitable ones. This sort of trial period of domesticity quickly weeds out those sites that are too damp, draughty, disturbed or unsuitable for some other reason. It is thought to be usually the male who makes the final choice of nest site, but once the eggs are laid, the female is very much the ruler of this domain.

She does the vast bulk of the incubation, if not all of it, leaving the nest only to exercise and drink. Normally the male will be fully occupied maintaining his territorial boundaries against his neighbours, who might well be keen to extend into some of his richer hunting areas. This territorial defence is often a very vigorous process, and a spine-chillingly vociferous one for the photographer closetted in his hide. Normally, too, the male will bring his incubating female all the food she needs, and sometimes more, in which case a ring of corpses will build up around her as she sits. Not until the chicks are old enough to be safely left alone will she join in hunting to help feed them, and even then her contributions will be brief as she makes frequent return visits to the nest to ensure its safety from predators.

The timing of breeding
In temperate regions, and even in more northerly cool-temperate zones, the breeding season begins early for owls, often in what we humans would quite validly call winter, with snow still on the ground. This pattern is so widespread and well established that it has obviously stood the test of time. Evolution has shown it to be the most effective: the hazards of chilling early-laid eggs must be more than offset by the benefits of hatching the young (and thus dramatically multiplying the food demands) at the time when the food supply is at its peak. Small birds and mammals, and many invertebrates, because of their size are quicker off the mark, when spring arrives, than the larger owls, and if the owls were not ready and waiting, the peak of food supply might pass untapped. Prey supplies usually remain at a high level during the summer months as the young owls grow in stature and hunting expertise. This is of great importance, as many of the bigger owl species may remain largely dependent on their parents for several months after they have fledged from the nest.

83

Top: *Uncomfortably propped up on her wings, a Short-eared Owl broods her young, who may well be too large or too active for such maternal attention.* Above, left: *Hatched eggshells left, rather conspicuously, at a Little Owl nest entrance. Most small song birds fly some distance away with their eggshells before dropping them.* Above, right: *An unusual Long-eared Owl nest site: on the ground and in a reed bed. It seems likely that these birds, abnormally, did do some actual nest building.*
Opposite: *A Little Owl, pupils widely dilated in the dark, pauses before dropping in to the nest hole with a large earthworm for the young.*

85

In the tropics, the pattern is rather different, as one might expect, but the general principle of gearing the reproductive cycle to the availability of food is maintained. The gentle seasonal gradation of climate is replaced by a pattern of wet and dry cycles during the year: the 'long' rains and the 'short' rains of East Africa, for example. The timing of the rains varies considerably from place to place, and indeed from year to year. The larger owls, seeking predominantly rodent prey, will have a breeding season timed so that their young extract major benefit from the 'bulge' in the rodent population in the dry season as the cereal and grass seeds ripen. These cereals and grasses will have stemmed from seeds germinated by the rains several weeks earlier.

In contrast, many of the primarily insectivorous owls will have young at times of peak insect numbers: this may, in tropical rain forests, be during the hot wet season. In the case of owls of more arid areas (like the Scops Owls of the Mediterranean basin) chicks may be produced at the height of the hot dry season when locusts, grasshoppers and the like are abundant.

Opposite, above: The young Snowy Owl's sooty down is in marked contrast to its parents' whiteness: perhaps the dark pigment helps absorb heat from the sun to keep the chick warm. Opposite, below: A young Eagle Owl, its drowsiness in the heat of the sun moderating its noble bearing. Before the feathers of the facial disc have developed to conceal it, the beak seems of a size appropriate to the owl's name.
Below: A family of young Barn Owls, using an old bullock skip basket for a home. Note the last signs of a vole being eaten by the nearest owlet.

87

*A juvenile Spotted Eagle Owl, with all its parents' fierce expression a little belied by its downy haircut.
Opposite, above: A parent Eagle Owl glares out from the rock sheltering its nest, whilst its young
concentrates actively on swallowing a nestling bird whole. Opposite, below: One of those warm afternoons.
The Short-eared Owl chick is fast asleep, and the eyelids of its brooding parent are clearly drooping.*

Clutch and brood sizes

Great variations in clutch (and subsequently brood) sizes from year to year and
place to place seem to be a characteristic feature of owls. They are one of the very few
groups of birds that seem able either to gauge the season's food supply in advance,
or adjust according to circumstances as the season develops. The tit family seem
able to gear their clutches to the caterpillar supply in the same sort of way, but most
other birds just seem to press on regardless, in effect overproducing eggs as a
safeguard against the probability that many will fail to be successfully reared.

Clutch size fluctuations are most notable in those owls which depend heavily on
small rodents for food. It is well known that rodent numbers, even here in temperate Europe but particularly noticeably in northern Europe and America in the
circumpolar tundra belt, rise and fall in a cyclic pattern, peaking roughly every four
years or so. In years of rodent peak numbers, the so-called vole- or lemming-
plagues, owl clutches will be very high. Particularly good examples are the Snowy
and Short-eared Owls, which in these conditions often lay ten eggs and sometimes
a dozen or even more. In the year that follows, rodent numbers will slump dramatically, and many of the owls lay only one or two eggs, or even none at all. To a greater
or lesser degree, depending on their diet, the clutch sizes of many other owls follow

88

similar patterns. In addition, there is a general and over-riding trend in owls (and other birds) of tropical regions to lay fewer eggs than those in temperate and cool-temperate latitudes.

The eggs are sometimes laid at daily intervals in smaller owls, but more commonly every two days and in the Eagle Owls sometimes up to four days apart. Again we can see a flexibility of production geared to climate: if there is a spell of weather that prevents good hunting, then the stream of eggs may be interrupted for a longer period. Incubation usually starts as soon as the first egg is laid (also in contrast to most small birds) but the Pygmy Owl is an exception, waiting until its clutch is complete before sitting. Size has a marked effect on the length of the incubation period, the smaller owls taking around three weeks, the larger ones four or five. Because of the staggered laying, and subsequently hatching, the owlets will be of different ages *and sizes*. This is important, as naturally the oldest and largest chick is fed first, and continues to dominate the queue for food until fully satisfied; then the other chicks get their turn, once again in order of size. Thus if the owls have over-estimated the food supply, or if this fails for some reason, the youngest chick (which is also the smallest and weakest) will perish. Often, as it becomes weaker, it may become yet another food item to help the oldest stay alive and well fed. If need be, this process can be repeated with the next smallest and so on. Although this may seem callous and be abhorrent to us, it does provide a most unusual but practical back-up mechanism for improving the parent owls' chances of fledging successfully at least some of their nestlings.

A young Little Owl, almost ready to fly, waits for food at the entrance of its rabbit-burrow nest hole.

When they emerge from the eggshell, the owlets are tiny, blind, naked and helpless, and are fed minute strips of flesh with extreme care and delicacy by the female, who dismembers prey brought to the nest by the male. The owlets grow quickly, and develop a dense coat of short white down. This is soon replaced by a longer, fluffier grey or brown set of down feathers, through which the proper feathers of the young owl's first year plumage will soon begin to emerge. Ground-nesting owls may leave the actual nest site after a couple of weeks – well before they can fly – and hide singly in the rough vegetation. In the case of the Short-eared Owl, I can remember the difficulties and frustration of trying to find owlets widely scattered in grass. Tree and hole-nesting owlets will also emerge before they can fly, and clamber about looking awkwardly teenage with some grown-up feathers, but still with many tufts of down! Coming out of the nest helps them find space to perform vigorous – and very necessary – wing-flapping exercises to get their muscles toned up for the first flight.

In the early stages, the young seem to human eyes to be excessively ugly and reptilian, but one of the fascinations to me of an extended period of night-shift work photographing a nest is that I can share in the parental delight as the down-covered young – all beaks and feet – gradually turn into replicas of their parents, immaculate, but with a few tufts and wisps of down here and there giving away their age. Although the parents normally quietly slip away as soon as they hear you coming, the well-grown youngsters are bold in self-defence, crouching, head weaving from side to side, bills snapping and hissing like snakes, with wings spreadeagled to

A Little Owl carrying an earthworm to its rabbit-burrow nest. Although Burrowing Owls almost always have subterranean nests, Little Owls quite commonly share this habit.

make themselves appear larger than life. Younger chicks may roll over on to their backs, greeting the intruding hand or camera with feet raised and talons spread wide and menacingly.

Fledging times vary widely between years and also between individual pairs, and this, too, is probably linked to fluctuations in food supply. In vole-plague years, a medium-sized Short-eared Owl brood of five chicks might fledge in as little as twenty days, a large brood taking rather longer at twenty-five days. In a poor vole year, the growth rate of any surviving owlet may be slow, and even a small brood might take a month to fledge.

Once the young have fledged, few owls abandon their broods as quickly as do most small birds. One brood a year is the routine for most owls although Barn and Short-eared Owls can again be an exception in good vole years and raise two broods. This means that for most owls, there are not the pressures to get on with the next clutch of eggs that face smaller birds. The extended period of parental care may run to two or three months, allowing the young owls time to master the skills of hunting which they must do before they can be truly independent.

The territory size of a parent pair of birds will vary with the circumstances, but in

Opposite, above left: *A Short-eared Owl feeding its nestling, nictitating membrane drawn partly across its eye. Note the white 'egg tooth' used to cut the egg membranes when the chick is hatching.* Opposite, above right: *Wing-stretching exercises for a young Short-eared Owl are vital for muscle development ready for flight.* Opposite, below: *Young Short-eared Owls leave the nest several days before they can fly.*
Below: *A Barn Owl returns to her nest in a Suffolk barn with a vole for her youngster.*

the case of the Tawny Owl living in oak woodland it may be as much as 20-30 hectares (50-70 acres). The young will be dotted about this territory, each at or near a regular 'feeding station' where its parents will know that it can be found. More often than not it will leave them in no uncertainty as to its whereabouts, 'ku-wek'ing noisily and hungrily from dusk onwards until the parents manage to satisfy its appetite. Gradually the youngsters will do more and more of their own hunting, until eventually dispersing and attempting to set up their own territories. This is undoubtedly the most hazardous period of their young lives, when food shortages, their own inexperience as hunters and a succession of failures to secure adequate feeding territory in competition with older established birds leads to a high juvenile mortality.

Nestboxes

In Europe, Barn Owls and Tawny Owls in particular will take readily to artificial nest sites of one sort or another, and Little Owls will sometimes occupy boxes designed for stock doves or jackdaws. Bearing in mind that the owls themselves do no nest building, and so often use a natural or man-made cavity or some other bird's cast-off nest, there seems no reason to suppose that other owls, across the world, might not be similarly tempted. Providing nestboxes, and getting them occupied

Part of one of the most thrilling sequences of my life, taken on Fetlar, Shetland Isles. Opposite, above: *The first Snowy Owl brood of six owlets. Note the great contrast in size and colour.* Opposite, below: *The male Snowy Owl selects suitable lookout posts from which to guard the nest.* Below: *The female Snowy Owl, her head feathers rather stained, broods well-grown young.*

95

Top: *The owlets having eaten their fill, the Fetlar Snowy Owl female stays beside her young to guard them.*
Above: *The same owl feeding an owlet with a pellet. Such re-use of the supposedly indigestible remains is not usual, and we must question whether any worthwhile nutritive value could be obtained in this way.*

A Tawny Owl nestbox – a simple but substantial wooden tube, fitted high on a suitable branch. Note the observation door and the drainage holes in the base.

by the desired species, is a fascinating challenge to the birdwatcher's ingenuity and ornithological knowledge, and most rewarding when success is achieved. If you live in or near Long-eared or Short-eared Owl habitat, you could try placing a flask-shaped structure with a side entrance (like the wickerwork duck nesting baskets that can be bought at country and gun shops) perhaps in a dense shrubby hawthorn or in tussocky long grass, and it may do the trick.

Suitable simple boxes for Barn and Tawny Owls are discussed on p. 102 and 126. Both these species (but the Tawny Owl in particular) will also use an old lidded barrel with a hole cut at the top of one stave for an entrance. Little Owls need much the same conditions, but with a smaller entrance hole – perhaps about 20 × 10 cm (8 × 4ins). Fortunately, nestboxes do not need to be master works of carpentry but they must be reasonably weather-proof and (very important) have good drainage at floor level. Siting is not difficult either, although here there is plenty of scope for experiment. They should be put up out of harm's way, which means sheltered from prevailing winds, direct sunlight and beating rains, and well out of reach of small boys. Sadly many children (and some of their elders) think that an owl would make a superbly unusual pet. This may be true, but attractive as owls undeniably are close-to, they are far more attractive, and effective, free in their natural habitat.

Owls in general are beneficial to man: none is positively harmful, and in several cases owls help to maintain at reasonably balanced and tolerable levels, troublesome animals, including pests like rats and mice. Man, in his search for progress and higher efficiency, often eliminates natural nest sites unthinkingly, so the provision of nestboxes is a very simple and useful return contribution for the benefits, and the pleasures, of owls' company.

The Tawny Owl in Close-up

Although some other owls will take up residence in the heart of our cities, the Tawny Owl seems paramount at exploiting this man-made niche. Its only near competitor is perhaps the Scops Owl, extremely inconspicuous visually, but 'poop'ing penetratingly through the warm evening air in many of the towns in Mediterranean Europe.

The Tawny Owl is ancestrally a bird of open woodland and forest glades, and indeed it is sometimes called the Wood Owl. Despite this, large, well-vegetated suburban gardens and even city-centre parks with an abundance of mature trees seem to serve the Tawny Owl equally well: perhaps they are regarded as isolated outposts of woodland. Clearly Tawny Owls have been making use of urban habitats for some time: for example, Gray (1716-71) in his *Elegy Written in a Country Churchyard* says

Save from yonder ivy-mantled tower
The moping owl doth to the moon complain

Tawny Owls are moderately large birds, standing about 35-40 cm (14-16 ins) high, and easily recognized even in silhouette by their dumpy outline and oversize round head. I always think that the flight silhouette is just as distinctive, or more so – the large round head seems to dwarf the body, and the wings are strikingly broad and rounded, with very distinctly 'fingered' ends.

The range of the Tawny Owl extends over much of Europe, from as far north as 65° (that is about the level of Iceland), south to the Mediterranean, North Africa and the Himalayas, and east to Siberia and China. Over much of this range, the Tawny Owl seems to choose as its habitat open broad-leaved woodland and forest, but particularly in the upland parts of its range, such as the Alps or Himalayas, the Tawny may also be a characteristic bird of tall conifer woodland. Even in Britain, many largely-coniferous plantations provide apparently perfectly adequate habitat.

Most often, Tawny Owls seek shelter from the brightness of daylight hours in cavities in little-used buildings, or more commonly in natural holes in trees. Where such holes are scarce, the Tawny Owl may rely on its fabulous camouflage, the

Opposite: *A portrait photograph of a Tawny Owl. As in so many owls, there are two colour phases: this one is rufous, but the other phase is much greyer.*

99

greys, buffs, chestnuts and blacks blending imperceptibly with a tree trunk if the owl remains motionless. If there is some ivy about to give additional shelter, so much the better. Although human eyes may regard this camouflage as near-perfect, more often than not my attention has been drawn to roosting Tawny Owls in woodland by the clamour raised by other birds that have spotted them. Chief amongst these, usually, are blackbirds and chaffinches, which quickly alert other birds to gather round and 'mob' the luckless owl. Noisiest of these protesters, in my experience, are always jays and mistle thrushes, which seem able to work themselves up into a raucous frenzy, often, in their excitement and annoyance, approaching dangerously within inches of the owl. Quite what is the purpose of this mobbing behaviour by small birds, nobody really seems certain. Obviously the racket quickly alerts most other birds to the presence of a danger, but it has also been suggested that the gathering of finches, thrushes and tits around an owl serves as a collective 'refresher course', schooling them all as to the owl's appearance should they not have seen one recently. A rough human equivalent would be a fire-drill practice following the sounding of the alarm.

The breeding season starts early for the Tawny Owl, and from October onwards the typical hooting 'hoo-hoo-hoo-hoo-hoooooo . . .' call can be heard through the night, the last phrase hanging on the air vibrantly before gradually fading. Much of this calling is due to males setting up their territorial boundaries, with challenge and counter challenge echoing across the woods. The females will respond usually with a sharp, quite different, 'kee-wick'. This calling continues right through the coldest nights of the winter, bringing home the truth of those super lines of William Shakespeare, in *Love's Labour's Lost*:

> *When icicles hang by the wall*
> *And Dick the shepherd blows his nail*
> *And Tom bears logs into the hall*
> *And milk comes frozen home in pail*
> *When blood is nipped and ways be foul*
> *Then nightly sings the staring owl*
> *Tu who, tu wit tu whoo – a merry note.*

In any woodland area, the number of pairs of owls can vary considerably from year to year, and even when numbers are reasonably static, there always seem to be demarcation disputes over the territorial limits, and the minor gains and losses in area are alway certain to generate considerable verbal abuse from neighbouring birds! One problem with watching or photographing owls, when you are out alone long after dark, is that their flight is so silent that they can approach quite close without your knowledge. An earsplitting series of hoots from just over your shoulder is quite enough to make your heart stand still!

During courtship, the male may chase his intended swiftly but silently through the trees, rarely even brushing a twig as he passes. Sometimes, though, I have

Opposite, above: *A typical Tawny nest site in a cleft tree. This bird has taken a small rabbit back to well-grown nestlings.* Opposite, below: *This bird is much more exposed in an extraordinary situation, relying on her camouflage against the leaf litter for protection.*

heard him give a series of 'wing claps' – not, as you might suppose, made as we clap our hands in applause, but caused by the flicking of the wing feathers in much the same way as the flick of a human wrist will cause a whip to crack. Once they are perched, the male will sidle up to the female, swaying slowly from side to side, bobbing up and down and raising one or both wings in slow motion in an ungainly but rather attractive gesture that I love to watch. At the same time he will raise and lower his body feathers to make himself appear first large, then small. Presumably this rather mesmeric performance, accompanied by subdued grunts and hoots, is designed to make the female more receptive to his advances.

Actual breeding also starts early: normally in southern Britain the Tawny Owl photographer should be active in March. The nest is usually in a cavity similar to that used for roosting, and in my experience many owls will select the most suitable of their winter roosts and use it for breeding. Occasionally other sites are used such as old squirrel dreys, or bulky but disused nests such as those of carrion crows or magpies. Fortunately Tawny Owls take readily to artificial sites like nestboxes. An old barrel with a hole cut in the side is an attractive nestbox, but more functional

Left and above: *This Tawny Owl is flying from its nest hole – an old rabbit burrow. The entrance to the nest can be clearly seen. Notice how the legs are long enough to have pushed the bird well into the air on take-off.*

ones can be simply made from four 23 cm (9 in.) planks about a metre long, cut and nailed together to form a square-section tube. A base made of small-mesh wire netting, or something similar, is essential to allow drainage, and the box is best slung at an angle beneath a suitable stout branch. Such boxes have been used extensively for research on Tawny Owls by Dr H.N. Southern and his colleagues at Oxford. Their work for the University at Wytham Wood has contributed in a very major way to our understanding of Tawny Owl behaviour and ecology.

There are a number of records of Tawny Owls nesting on the ground, especially in conifer plantations, where after the lower branches have been lopped off, a dense tangle of branches covers the forest floor, providing a suitable structure and shelter and concealment for the nest and the sitting bird. Such a choice of nest sites allows scope for Tawny Owls to nest at a considerable range of heights, and although most are probably within 6-8 metres (20-25 feet) of the ground, those in old towers, dreys

Top left: *An unusually open Tawny nest, on the ground at the base of a tree trunk.* Top right: *Tawny Owl eggs in a ground nest of oak leaves.* Above: *The adult Tawny instinctively closes her eyes as an enthusiastic youngster rushes forward to grab the vole she is carrying.*
Opposite: *A young Tawny, still covered in down.*

106

From right to left: A Tawny Owl obligingly accepts an offering of bait left on a convenient tree stump. The owl approaches with its wings spread and tail fanned to fullest extent, braking in mid-air. The legs move into position for a quick strike, the talons widely spread. With eyes closed for protection, the bird seizes the bait.
Opposite, below: Tawny Owls are occasionally seen in farm outbuildings.

or nests may easily be 20 metres (65 feet) up – not an attractive prospect to the intending photographer.

It is probably now well known to most people that many years ago, when I was climbing up the pylon hide that my friend Cyril Newberry and I had erected to photograph a Tawny Owl in Wales, the female suddenly and silently attacked me. A talon lacerated my cheek, and as ill-luck would have it, penetrated my left eye. Despite a furious dash back across the country to Moorfields Eye Hospital in London, it proved impossible to save the eye. This was well before the days of fast-acting modern antibiotics, and I had to face the doubly agonizing decision whether to have the damaged eye removed, or leave it and risk infection and losing the sight of both my eyes. With the knowledge that two of the great early bird photographers, Walter Higham and Geoffrey Ingram, each had only one eye, and that a photographer essentially only needs one eye for his viewfinder, I chose the former course. I have always considered that the owl was only 'doing its duty' and protecting its nest, and so attach absolutely no blame to it. Indeed, even from such ill-fortune some good eventually came: how else would Frank Lane, my co-author, have arrived at such a wonderful title for my autobiography, as *An Eye for a Bird* (published in 1970 by Hutchinson)?

My experience should, though, serve as a warning to all naturalists, whether photographers, bird ringers or simply birdwatchers interested in seeing the nest

107

Top left and above: *Two pylon hides erected at Tawny Owl nesting sites. The photograph of the two young Tawnies (top right) clambering about near the nest was taken from the lower of the two hides (as was the top photograph on page 101).*

Top: *Huge dark eyes and the bristly feathers that make up the facial disc can be clearly seen in this Tawny Owl portrait.* Above, left: *The velvety upper surface of a Tawny Owl wing. The comb-like fringe on the leading edge helps break the air-flow over the wing for additional silencing.* Above, right: *A complete Tawny Owl pellet, and alongside, the typical collection of long bones, ribs, vertebrae and upper and lower jaws (with teeth) that can be extracted from it.*

109

and its contents. Many of our larger birds, not just the eagles, falcons, hawks and owls, but others such as the big gulls and the skuas (and even the comparatively diminutive Arctic tern) can be very determined and aggressive near their nests – often with painful results for the intruder and occasionally with tragic consequences. They should be treated with appropriate caution, forethought, and respect.

A quick glance at the short round wings should tell us that Tawny Owls use a very different hunting technique from, say, Short-eared Owls or Barn Owls. Long wings and extended food-searching flights are perhaps far from ideal for hunting in woodland. Often, the Tawny Owl will remain perched on a branch overlooking the woodland floor, motionless apart from scanning movements as the head turns to pinpoint, by sight or sound, some movement on the ground below. Once the target prey is located, the Tawny will drop silently, talons outstretched, either vertically or in a steep glide. The broad round wings can then be used to best effect – held cupped, rather like a parachute, to slow and control its plunge.

The long-term studies by research workers at Oxford University showed that although the diet of the Tawny Owls in Wytham Wood consisted largely of small rodents, especially bank voles and long-tailed fieldmice, there was ample evidence of versatility. In these studies and others, over twenty different types of mammal and over forty different species of birds (ranging in size from the tiny goldcrest to an astonishingly large mallard) have been recorded in the Tawny Owl diet over the years. There is no way of cataloguing satisfactorily the many beetles, snails, slugs and worms that we know they will eat when other larger foods are scarce. Tawny Owls with territories close to water will take frogs and fish, and (no doubt much to man's annoyance) even trout. In suburban areas, handsomely plump goldfish are on record as victims!

Woodland Tawny Owls have a diet of roughly ninety per cent rodents and ten per cent birds, while in towns this situation is almost exactly reversed. Not surprisingly, in urban areas house sparrows and starlings are the main dietary items, the rodent component being largely rats and house mice.

Tawny Owls attract me all the more by their capability to coexist with man and their ability to exploit man-made environments. This ability conveys hidden benefits, because in towns as well as in woods, they are often insulated from most aspects of toxic pollution generated by man that would be harmful to them: the sad impact of pesticides on the largely-agricultural Barn Owl underlines this point. Their versatility in diet and habitat also allows them to avoid the worst impact of periods of severe weather, and with such catholic tastes, it is hardly to be wondered at that Tawny Owls are such successful birds.

Opposite: *Although taking owls specially to make them into pets is illegal, Tawny Owls readily become domesticated, sharing an eagerness to be first to the daily paper and concerned for the day's weather.*

The Barn Owl in Close-up

More often than not, most of us will see Barn Owls after dark. I can remember on many occasions being startled when driving at night when what seemed to be one of the white road-marking lines suddenly took wing! In the brightness of car headlights, Barn Owls appear glaringly white and obvious, but despite this, the speed of modern cars and the owls' relatively slow flight result in a great many casualties. Studies of recoveries of ringed birds show that cars (and trains) are sadly one of the major causes of Barn Owl deaths.

To the solitary walker in a poorly-lit country lane – perhaps with the moon coming and going behind the clouds – a ghostly white apparition, moving on silent wings but occasionally emitting soul-in-torment shrieks, could easily conjure up the spirit world. Couple this with their habit of living and hunting around ruined buildings and churchyards, and Barn Owls immediately become likely contenders as the origins of many ghost stories, re-told, each time with additional embellishment, in the village pub.

Perhaps more than any other owl, the Barn Owl gets closest to the Hosking family's heart. I think they are lovely creatures, and now David too has great difficulty resisting any opportunity to photograph them. Everybody seems to be fascinated by Barn Owls, a fact reflected by the simple commercial statistics that of all the birds I have photographed, it is the Barn Owl that is most often reproduced. Moreover, my best-selling single photograph, in terms of numbers, is surely the one of the Barn Owl approaching its nest, with a vole in its beak and its wings set in an heraldic (almost angelic) posture. No wonder Dorothy frequently wears the simple brooch designed from this photograph, its tiny jewelled eyes reflecting the light in a way that reminds me very much of the real owl.

At first glance, a perched Barn Owl appears slightly top-heavy. The head is large and rounded, the face characteristically heart-shaped, and the body tapers away to a pair of long, slightly knock-kneed legs, covered in white feathers down onto the feet. The stance is almost always upright. A closer view shows that the apparently sandy back is a wonderful mixture of subtle browns, greys, buffs and beiges. The face is always white, but the various races of Barn Owl to be found round the world have very different coloured breasts. In Britain and western Europe, the majority

Opposite: *It seems difficult to imagine, but this beautifully marked spread of wings* can *be folded and compressed enough for the Barn Owl to slip easily into its nest hole.*

113

In close-up, the full and fine detail of the bristly feathers of the facial disc is revealed.
Opposite, below: A typical 'Barn-Owl-barn'. The owl pictured above entered through the missing shutter,
and its regular perching brick can be seen on the sill. Opposite, above left: The male Barn Owl pauses
briefly on his return. The prey is a common shrew. Opposite, above right: Hunting at dusk as well as by
night, this time the owl has caught a half-grown rat, which has been decapitated.

are white (or pale-) breasted, with very few brown spots; elsewhere they may be white, or heavily peppered with spots, or shaded through to deep chestnut as in the so called 'dark-breasted' form from northern and eastern Europe.

The Barn Owl is by no means exclusively nocturnal, and can often be seen hunting as daylight fades. In winter, when days are short and nights long and cold, and particularly when there is a covering of snow, feeding time is at a premium and owls may be seen on the wing hunting right through the day. When snow covers the long grass, the small rodents that the Barn Owls are seeking can scamper about their business in their runs, insulated and certainly not hampered by the snow, which conceals them most effectively from their enemies. At such times life is really hard for Barn Owls, and extended periods of snow cause heavy mortality. After a savage winter like that of 1962-63, it took the British Barn Owl population several years to recover to anything like normality.

Barn Owls do a lot of daylight feeding, too, when both parents are busy hunting flat out to feed a growing brood of youngsters, and this is especially true in those years when brood sizes are large. The hunting technique seems to be similar day or night, winter or summer.

114

Soft lighting brings out to the full the subtle colours and patterns of the Barn Owl's plumage.
Opposite, above: *Crisp in every detail, the Barn Owl begins to brake for its approach to the nest, a vole in its beak. The reflectors on either side of the picture are two high-speed flash lamps.* Opposite, below: *The vole swings like a pendulum as the owl turns for its final approach.*

The long and narrow wings indicate a relatively sophisticated flight pattern. Like the Short-eared Owl and the harrier family, the Barn Owl is a searcher/hunter, covering large areas of open ground in a search for food. The flight is lazily flapping, alternating with short glides on outstretched wings. The search is so methodical and to a pattern that it is called 'quartering', and man himself has had to devise similar effective searching patterns, for example, when an air-sea rescue aircraft is seeking a lost yacht in mid-ocean.

World-wide, Barn Owls hunt over open farmland, meadows and hillside rough grazing grassland, extending their operations onto commons and moors, and marshland fringes. In many areas they will hunt over broken scrub, and even on the edges of the desert areas of Africa, Asia and Australia, which support good small mammal populations – certainly more than adequate to tempt Barn Owls.

Most often, prey is seized on the ground with a sudden swoop or plunge. This is

117

The Barn Owl departs, swooping down from the nest hole to gain flying speed.
Opposite, above: Wings spread to their fullest extent, the owl speeds away from the nest.
Opposite, below: Arriving on a beam above the nest, this owl's prey (a vole) is ready for transfer to the beak
(left); *once transferred to the beak* (centre), *the vole can be more easily fed to the young;* (right) *a shrew is
held in the beak for presentation to the owlets.*

where the length of leg is put to good effect, as the luckless mouse can be grabbed without the wings coming into contact with nearby vegetation and causing a crash-landing! Once caught, there is little chance of escape.

As with most other owls, Barn Owl diets tend to vary with habitat and time of year, with most birds taking advantage of any local abundance of suitable food and relatively few being at all choosy in their choice of meals. So Barn Owls, although over most of their range concentrating on rodents (or similar animals – for example small marsupials in Australasia) ranging in size from tiny harvest mice up to rats, will readily eat other animals, even as lowly as earthworms and large insects. They will readily eat shrews – not often a favoured dietary item – but in Britain the remains most commonly found in pellets are of bank and short-tailed voles, long-tailed fieldmice and house mice. Near marshes, they will take frogs and even fish occasionally, and should there be a roost of smaller birds in their hunting area, then birds will feature regularly in the diet. Usually the roosting birds (ranging in size from the commonly-caught house sparrow up to the blackbird) are snatched from their perches, but there are records of Barn Owls beating bushes with their wings to disturb their prey.

In one British Barn Owl territory, I remember there was a huge roost of pied

119

An interesting shot of a Barn Owl, legs extended for landing, braking as she approaches the nest. Opposite, above: Under full braking, even the alula, or 'bastard wing' (a group of feathers attached to the owl's 'thumb') can be seen extended on the leading edge of the wing to help slow her down. Normally, the alula functions as do the 'slots' in a modern aircraft wing, helping to improve the airflow over the upper surface at low speeds. Opposite, below left: Owl eggs are far rounder than those of most birds, and the Barn Owl's are no exception. The chalky-white eggshell shown here is stained from contact with the nest, which is no more than a layer of bits of straw and old pellets. Opposite, below right: Although these Barn Owl chicks are over three weeks old, there is still little sign of their proper feathers emerging through the dense white down.

A hide comfortably and conveniently set up in the corner of a Norfolk barn. The Barn Owls shown opposite were nesting in the topmost withy bullock skip, behind the shafts of the cart.
Opposite, above: *Inside the bullock skip nest: a young rat is brought to the owlets.*
Opposite, below: *Notice how the facial discs of all four owlets are fully developed, while on only one have the wing feathers replaced the down.*

123

Left: *With wings caught almost in a vertical plane by the electronic flash, the Barn Owl begins to slow down as it approaches its nest.* Right: *Undercarriage down, the Barn Owl prepares to land.*
Opposite: *Although these young Barn Owls are much the same size, the age differences are given away by the varying quantity of down.*

wagtails in an enormous, and of course heated, horticultural glasshouse. The ventilator windows were closed automatically by a thermostat as the temperature fell, and on occasion the pied wagtails (leaving their feeding and moving off to roost at dusk) were caught out by the sudden descent of the chill of evening closing the vents. On such occasions the late-comers – and on most evenings some birds were tardy – had to roost under the eaves. Now Barn Owls are sufficiently astute hunters to discover this quickly, and using (once again) the long reach of their legs, were easily able to steal a pied wagtail from its perch.

In reasonable weather, Barn Owls roost during the day in suitably sheltered and dark places, similar to and very often the same as their nest sites. Sometimes this may be a natural cavity in a rock face, or rather more often a hollow in a tree, usually where a branch has broken off. Man provides many other sites. The best-known are church towers, ruined buildings and barns, but almost any deserted or little-used building will suffice. One of the sadder aspects of modern farming (to the conservationist) is the removal of so many of these eminently suitable old tree stumps and the demolition of tumbledown barns, windmills and old cottages. Hedgerow trees are not normally replaced, so the roost or nest site is lost. Barns are replaced, but with sterile, corrugated-asbestos structures, which are airy and well-lit and totally alien to Barn Owl needs.

Fortunately the farming community is well aware of the benefits of the Barn Owl as an unpaid rodent operative – to use the modern job-description for rat-catcher. With a little thought, publicity and persuasion, farmers are ready, sometimes with the help of local naturalists, to darken one corner of a new barn and provide an

124

Emerging from a hollow-tree nest site, the flash reveals that this Barn Owl is blind from a cataract in the left eye, possibly arising from an old injury.

entrance hole leading to a very simple nestbox. This can be just a platform, or a shallow box about 60 cm (2 feet) square and 30 cm (1 foot) deep, possibly roofed over and with its own entrance hole in a corner if the barn is not dark enough. Fortunately, in my experience the owls respond most rewardingly by readily occupying the new premises.

I have already mentioned that Barn Owl populations suffer badly in hard winters, in collisions with cars, and (indirectly) by loss of habitat as economic pressures force farmers to increase productivity and modernize their operations. All over northern Europe in the last thirty years, considerable fluctuations in Barn Owl numbers have been recorded by ornithologists, and although some recovery usually follows disaster, the overall trend is still downwards. Sadly, Barn Owls did not escape contamination (through their food chain) by some of the newer, more toxic and more persistent organochlorine pesticides, the use of which is now, fortunately, largely banned or very restricted. The Tawny Owl, as a woodland and urban bird, largely escaped this hazard.

Top: *The contented chicks doze while their mother does her best to brood them in their untidy heap.*
Above: *An embarrassment of riches: male and female have returned simultaneously to the nest with food. Only one owlet seems at all interested, and even it appears to be falling asleep over its meal.*

The lowered head and extended, drooped wings indicate an aggressive display.
Opposite: Especially in winter, Barn Owls regularly hunt in daylight, often pausing to scan for potential prey.

Particularly in Europe, the Barn Owl and man are closely linked in many ways. There can be no question of the popularity and attraction of the Barn Owl to the general public, nor indeed is there much doubt that the agricultural community recognize Barn Owls as valuable components of the countryside, with a very positive contribution to make in the overall regulation of the numbers of harmful small rodents. Farmer, financier, industrialist and conservationist must combine in endeavours to provide a secure future for this elegant owl, so much a feature of our farmscape.

A Gallery of Owls

The Galapagos Short-eared Owl – as tame and approachable as most of the animals on this remote group of islands, 700 miles west of Ecuador in the Pacific Ocean. What better example could one choose of the immensely far-flung range of the Short-eared Owl, which includes many similarly isolated mid-oceanic islands?

Opposite: The conspicuous feather tufts on the top of the head – the origin of the Long-eared Owl's name – have nothing to do with hearing. They are thought to play a subtle role in display and individual recognition. Long-eared Owls are widely distributed in open woodland in North America, Europe, Asia and parts of Africa. The very finely marked plumage offers the roosting bird excellent camouflage against a tree trunk during the day, when the eyelids of the resting bird will droop and the feathers of its facial disc will close to improve its concealment.

The African Marsh Owl in many ways resembles the Short-eared Owl (opposite) and is more or less its ecological equivalent over much of Africa. It is an owl of open grasslands, particularly marshy areas, nesting on the ground under a grassy tunnel. When they are about half-grown the youngsters move away from the nest and remain in individual concealment nearby. Unlike the Short-eared Owl, it has a pale patch which shows up in the wing when in flight, and rather than concentrate on hunting voles in daylight, the African Marsh Owl feeds mostly on large insects caught after dark.

Opposite: The Short-eared Owl has one of the widest ranges of all the owls, spanning the globe in both hemispheres. A daylight hunter and very much a bird of open country – marsh, moor or steppe – it is readily recognized by its long-winged, laboured, jerky flight and by the dark patches at the angle (or wrist) of each wing.

In characteristic upright posture on an exposed perch, the Little Owl is the best-known small (22cm/9ins) owl of Europe and Asia. Its familiarity to man stretches back at least to early civilizations in Athens, and no wonder, as it is extremely catholic in its choice of habitat and in its diet, thriving successfully in farmland and in towns. Contrary to popular belief, it is not a true native of Britain, having become established only after several attempts at introduction during the nineteenth century.

The Spotted Little Owl, with its white-spectacled eyes, is slightly smaller than the Little Owl of Europe. It is a common bird in open woodland of many sorts, but penetrates farmland and plains, and even city parks and large gardens. In habits and in habitat it seems to take over (in ecological terms), in the Middle East and southeast Asia, where the Little Owl leaves off.

135

Dramatically spectacular in every aspect, the Eagle Owl of Europe must be one of the most striking birds in the world. Its fearsome appearance and flaming eyes are matched by its size (up to 70cm/28ins) and by its hunting capabilities. With the full force of a swoop behind them, those huge talons can bring down and kill a small deer.

Opposite: The Eurasian Eagle Owl has a tremendous range, so variations in size and colour are to be expected. One of the most distinct races (so much so that some authorities feel that it should be a species in its own right) is the Pharaoh or Desert Eagle Owl. As might be expected from its habitat – arid scrub and scattered trees on rocky outcrops in desert areas of the Middle East – the Pharaoh Eagle Owl is a pale sandy fawn, but more surprising, it is little more than half the size of the largest Eagle Owls from the boreal forests of high latitudes.

137

The Abyssinian Eagle Owl – one of the races of the Spotted Eagle Owl occurring north of the equator – can be distinguished from Spotted Eagle Owls from further south by its pale plumage and dark eyes. This bird is beginning to take up a threatening posture. The wings are extended and drooped, the bird is crouching slightly and has opened up its voluminous and very delicate body feathers.

Opposite: The Turkestan Eagle Owl is an excellent example of how pale and grey are the Eurasian Eagle Owl races from very dry areas in the south and east of the species' range. These birds are also smaller than those from northern Europe, often standing a few inches shorter than their relatives at about 58cm (23ins).

Mackinder's Eagle Owl is a spectacular and distinct race of the Cape Eagle Owl of Africa, restricted to a few highland areas mainly from Kenya south to Zimbabwe. It is a large (48cm/19ins) and heavily marked Eagle Owl, feeding mainly on small mammals, and roosting during the day in the gnarled and grotesque lichen-shrouded trees of these isolated mountain areas.

Opposite: *The Spotted Eagle Owl occurs throughout Africa south of the Sahara Desert, preferring open bush country and lightly-wooded hills. As Eagle Owls go, it is small, rarely reaching 40cm (16ins), and perhaps because of this large insects feature greatly in its diet, supplementing the more usual small birds and mammals. Not only are there two colour phases – one greyish, the other brown – but there are also two well-defined races – northern and southern – with the boundary between the two more or less running along the equator. The northern form tends to be greyer, with fewer spots and with brown eyes, rather than the striking yellow of this southern bird.*

141

The Nduk Eagle Owl is a small (40cm/16ins), dark-eyed Eagle Owl with very bold markings. The Nduk Eagle Owl is the name given to an extraordinary race, isolated in Tanzania, of Fraser's Eagle Owl from the equatorial rainforests of West Africa. Because of their scarcity and the difficulties of penetrating their inhospitable environment, little is known of their biology.

142

The Cape Eagle Owl, as its name suggests, comes from southern Africa but ranges northwards into the Ethiopian highlands. It could equally well have been called the Mountain Eagle Owl, as open mountain forests are its exclusive habitat.

The Verreaux's (or Milky) Eagle Owl is a very large owl (60cm/24ins), taking hares, hyraxes and large birds like francolins and guinea fowl. Perhaps in this way it avoids competition with the smaller Spotted Eagle Owl, which has much the same wide distribution over Africa south of the Sahara Desert. Verreaux's Eagle Owls love to roost during the day in the tall yellow-barked Acacias characteristic of meandering watercourses. A close-up view of this pale, milky-white owl (hence the alternative name) would show that the eyelids, when closed, are a conspicuous and most unexpected bright pink.

Opposite: *Huge size and a generally dark appearance, with particularly bold markings, indicate that this race of the Great Horned Owl should come from forest at one extreme or the other of the species' range: birds from central America and drier habitats are small and pale. This is in fact the Magellan Eagle Owl, from the tail end of the Andes in extreme South America.*

145

Opposite and above: *Large (50cm/20ins) and powerful, the Great Horned Owl has an impressive range, stretching from the boreal conifer forests of Canada and Alaska southwards to the extreme tip of South America. Habitats include mountain forests, deciduous woodland, rainforest, swamps, deserts, prairies and mountain ranges bereft of trees. The Great Horned Owl favours various types of hare as a major source of food and needs a large territory – often several square miles – so that it can glean enough food in lean years. The owl on the left is in full cry. The call, uttered in a series of several hoots, carries for a great distance and is very deep-throated and mournful.*

The oversize, globular head and the facial expression of permanent surprise make the African Wood Owl easy
to recognize. The only member of their genus to be found in the Old World, they are reasonably common in
African woodlands south of the Sahara Desert. They prefer the dense growth alongside rivers, especially for
roosting during the day, but will range widely in search of food. Their diet is as varied as that of the Tawny
Owl, including small mammals, birds, insects and even reptiles.

Opposite: When it is not busily 'inflating' its image to try to intimidate the photographer, the Barking Owl
looks remarkably hawk-like, with a long tail and a most un-owl-like head, almost entirely lacking the usual
markings round the eyes and the facial disc of bristly feathers. It is a medium-sized owl (40cm/16ins) from
rather dry, sparse forest and bush country in Australasia, feeding largely on rabbits and large birds.
Unusually for owls, and indeed most birds of prey, the male is appreciably larger than the female.

150

The Collared Scops Owl is currently one of the most successful owls. Confined to east and southeast Asia, it favours open woodland and farmland, and thus is benefiting as more and more forest vanishes, converted often into very poor farmland. Clearly a Scops in appearance and size, the plumage colour of the Collared Scops varies relatively little compared with its European relative, and its call, a mournful whistle, is just as regularly repeated but at long time-intervals.

Opposite: Strikingly hawk-like in appearance, but with a reasonably prominent facial disc pattern, this Powerful Owl gives a clear indication of why the group of owls to which it belongs acquired the collective name 'hawk owls'. Indeed this species is sometimes called the Great Hawk Owl. An inhabitant of densely forested ravines in the coastal belt of south and east Australia, the Powerful Owl is, as its name suggests, among the larger owls at 65cm (26ins). Although dissimilar in shape, they are the Antipodean ecological equivalent of the Barred Owl of the New World and the Ural Owl of the Old. Powerful Owls nest in holes high up in very substantial trees and rarely do they lay more than two eggs. They have an unusual diet, including birds, arboreal marsupials like the opossum and gliding pouched animals like the flying fox and flying squirrel.

151

The Seychelles Bare-legged Scops Owl almost literally came back from the dead. Given up as extinct for many years, a tiny population was rediscovered in 1959 in the hills on the island of Mahe, where the distinctive 'tock, tock' call is often the only clue to their presence. This is one member of a small group of Scops Owls on the islands of the western side of the Indian Ocean, regarded by some authorities as separate species, by others just as insular races of the Madagascan Scops Owl.

Opposite: Neat and distinctive, the Eastern Screech Owl could be called the typical owl of North America. Widespread over that continent, Eastern Screech Owls are renowned for their aggression, especially in defence of their nests. Intending photographers should beware: although less than 22cm (10ins) tall, the Eastern Screech Owl can attack with all the fury of an airborne wildcat!

The unfeathered legs of the Rufous Fishing Owl, and its powerful feet, with knobbly skin to give a good grip on slippery prey, more resemble those of an osprey than of most owls. The large, powerful beak is osprey-like too. This is a handsome owl, about 50cm (20ins) tall, from the rainforests of tropical West Africa. Very little is known of its biology or ecology, and although it is obviously well adapted to catch fish, many questions remain unanswered — for example, how does it locate its underwater prey in the fading light? Other Fishing Owls, though also fish-catching specialists, are known to augment their diet with a wide variety of amphibians, reptiles, birds and small mammals.

Opposite: *The Vermiculated Fishing Owl is restricted to the edges of rivers in the forests of tropical West and Central Africa. The powerful unfeathered talons and legs, typical of a fishing owl, can be seen clearly, as can the deep fish-slicing beak. We know little of its habits save that it hunts at night and will take other prey besides fish.*

155

By far the most terrestrial of all the owls, the Burrowing Owl of the Americas lives on open treeless plains.
Superficially similar to the Little Owl in looks and behaviour, it has considerably longer legs and runs about
very nimbly. Although capable of excavating its own burrow, the Burrowing Owl more often commandeers a
disused rodent burrow, and there will roost and breed. The breeding chambers of prairie dogs make ideal nest
sites, and are up to one metre below the ground. Often several pairs of owls will gather into a loose colony to
take advantage of extensive prairie dog excavations. Not surprisingly for an owl that hunts on foot in hot, dry
habitats, the Burrowing Owl feeds largely on insects – especially beetles – with the occasional unwary small
rodent or reptile thrown in.
Opposite: *The Rusty-barred (or Brazilian) Owl is a woodland bird, roughly similar to the Tawny Owl in size*
and to some extent in appearance. Apparently confined to Brazil, as its name implies, it is one of many owls
about which we know very little, despite the fact that several are in captivity around the world.

The Barred Owl of eastern North America is capable of hunting its prey by sound in absolute total darkness under laboratory experimental conditions. Although this individual is obviously in captivity, in the wild it is one of the most strictly nocturnal of owls, so such skill is perhaps not too surprising though it does also make use of exceptional poor-light vision. It is a huge, round-headed owl up to 60cm (24ins) high, predominantly of damp mature forests, usually nesting in an old hollow tree or a large disused nest. These Barred Owl nest sites may be used regularly for many years in succession. The hooting call is among the more complex of owl songs, roughly similar in structure and nature to that of the Tawny Owl but baritone to the Tawny's tenor. American field guides often transliterate it as 'who cooks for you, who cooks for you all'.

Opposite: *The Spotted Wood Owl is distinguished from its relatives in India and southeast Asia by the white marks visible on its forehead. Despite its size (standing about 50cm/19ins tall) it feeds almost exclusively on large beetles. It is a strictly nocturnal-hunting owl and lives in open woodland and farmland in the Malaysian lowlands.*

159

The Northern Hawk Owl is the most northerly representative of the hawk owl group. It is a daytime hunter, sitting on prominent vantage points and swooping swiftly, almost like a sparrowhawk, onto its prey – usually mice, voles or lemmings. It is a bird of conifer and birch forests in the far north of Eurasia and Canada, and although sharing the hawk-like silhouette of the hawk owls of Australasia and the Orient, is only distantly related, if at all. The most obvious difference is the far more owl-like face of the Northern Hawk Owl, with conspicuous markings on the facial disc – vastly different from the Ninox group.

Opposite: This Barn Owl was photographed in Australia. Only a critically discerning eye would notice the rather brownish-grey back to the Australian race compared with the more chestnut mantle of pale-breasted Barn Owls from Europe or North America. Strangely, despite the Barn Owl's natural 'invasion' and colonization of Australia (thought to be from India via the Malay Peninsula and the island chain stretching southeast), and despite the tendency of early settlers to try to establish familiar birds from 'home' in their new country, there have been only a handful of records of Barn Owls from New Zealand.

162

Opposite, above: *One of the most southerly Barn Owl races, the African Barn Owl from South Africa is slightly larger than its European and American counterparts.*

Above and opposite, below: *The knock-kneed appearance and heart-shaped face suggest that the Masked Owl of Australasia is related to the Barn Owl. It is the largest of the Tyto owls and at about 50cm (20ins) tall, as big as many of the Eagle Owls. Possibly because of its large size, it is nowhere particularly common, which is a little surprising as its major prey in many areas is the exceedingly numerous rabbit. It is an open forest bird, often roosting during the day (and nesting) in large, hollow eucalyptus trees. There are several species from various islands, and each has both pale and dark phases. The pale phase shown above has a whitish facial disc, that of the dark phase (see left) being reddish buff. The dark-phase bird on the left is in a threatening pose.*

Owls in Camera

The cameras I used in the early days were the Sanderson Field, the Soho Reflex and the Brand 17. The latter was a lightweight, all-metal camera produced in the United States which had almost the same range of movements as the Sanderson but which could also be used in the hand. All these cameras were quarter-plate (4¼'' × 3¼'') in size, and were used with either glass plates or film packs (a number of thin sheets of film held in a metal container which were changed by pulling on a paper tag; they saved the weight and bulk of plate holders).

In the early days the material used was orthochromatic (not sensitive to red light) and I preferred Ilford's 'Golden Iso Zenith' plates. Later on in 1934 their 'Soft Gradation Pan' plate, which was sensitive to all colours, became available, and I used these together with Kodak's P800 plates, introduced in 1938, changing to their faster P1200 in 1946. The film packs were usually Kodak Super-XX but I also used Tri-X and Verichrome Pan.

In 1946 the Sashalite flash bulbs were replaced by the high-speed flash electronic unit with a flash duration of 1/5000th of a second and this has now been replaced by our Braun set-up which gives a duration of 1/10,000th.

The Contax camera was fitted with a coupled rangefinder which worked with lenses up to 135mm in focal length; 'reflex housing' was used with longer lenses. When the Contarex appeared in 1963 I adopted this 'pentaprism reflex' with its range of superb lenses. The 35mm films I used were Kodak's Panatomic-X, Plus-X and Tri-X for black and white work and, for colour, Kodachrome.

Previously, just after the war, I had used 'Sheet Kodachrome' in quarter-plate size, but it had to be returned to the United States for processing; Kodachrome 2 was replaced by Kodachrome 25, and we also used Kodachrome 64, Ektachrome 200 and 400.

The Hasselblad outfit was acquired in 1970 to obtain 2¼'' square transparencies, normally being used with 150mm and 250mm Zeiss Sonnar lenses and the 350mm and 500mm Tele-Tessars. Ektachrome film of various speeds was used.

Eventually we went over to colour transparency work entirely; if black and white prints are needed they are made from transparencies by making a negative.

Our 'Standard Zoo Technique' consists of using the Hasselblad with a 150mm Sonnar lens, with the addition of a 2M close-up lens. A Braun F700 flash

unit is connected to three extension heads, giving a flash duration of about 1/2000th of a second. Using Ektachrome 64, a stop midway between f11 and f16 (f12.5) is normally used.

The Contarex outfit has been replaced by Olympus OM-2n cameras with a variety of Zuiko lenses of different focal lengths. The OM-2n has an 'automatic shutter' – the stop is set and the camera automatically uses the right shutter speed in most situations. There is an 'over-ride' which allows you to increase or decrease the automatic exposure in certain circumstances. This camera is used with an Olympus T32 flash which gives the correct exposure without the need for Guide Numbers.

Key to abbreviations

Auto	Automatic Shutter Speed
E200	Ektachrome 200
E64	Ektachrome 64
EX	Ektachrome X
GIZ	Ilford Golden Iso Zenith
HSF	High Speed Flash 1/5000th flash duration
HSF-B	High Speed Flash 8 × Braun 280 flash heads 1/10,000th duration
K64	Kodachrome 64
KX	Kodachrome X
QPSR	Quarter-plate Soho Reflex
SFC	Sanderson Field Camera
SGP	Ilford Soft Gradation Pan
SZT	Standard Zoo Technique = Hasselblad, 150mm Sonnar lens, E64, f12.5, Braun 700 flash with three heads
THC	Taylor, Hobson, Cooke
TPQPR	Thornton Pickard Quarter-plate Reflex

Page

frontispiece *Barn Owl* Hasselblad, 80mm Planar, f12.5, HSF-B, E200, Devon, 1980 (David Hosking)

4-5 *Snowy Owl and young* Contarex, 250mm Sonnar, f5.6, 1/500th, Pan-X, Shetlands, 1967

12 *Tawny Owl* SFC, 21cm Tessar, f16, Sashalite flashbulb, SGP, Radnorshire (now Powys), 1938

13 *Barn Owl* SFC, 8½'' Dallmeyer Serrac, f16, Sashalite flashbulb, SGP, Suffolk, 1936

14 *Barn Owl* Olympus OM-2n, 100mm Zuiko, f11, T32 flash, K64, Falconry Centre, Gloucestershire, 1980 (David Hosking)

16 *Tawny Owl* Hasselblad, 150mm Sonnar, f12.5, HSF-B, E200, Buckinghamshire, 1980

17 *Tawny Owl* As page 16

18 *Rufous Owl* Olympus OM-2n, 300mm Zuiko, f4.5, T32 flash, K64 Burleigh Bird Sanctuary, Queensland, Australia

19 *Barn Owl* Brand 17, 21cm Tessar, f16, HSF, Tri-X, Suffolk, 1948

20 *Tengmalm's Owls* Contax, 135mm Sonnar, f5.6, 1/125th, Pan-X, Finland, 1958

22 *Greek vase and Owl* Mansell Collection, no details

23 *Spotted Eagle Owl* no details

25 *Burrowing Owl* SZT, London Zoo, 1981

26 *Tawny Frogmouth* Olympus OM-2n, 180mm Zuiko, f4, T32 fill-in flash, K64, Featherdale Bird Gardens, New South Wales, Australia
Nightjar Brand 17, 21cm Tessar, f16, HSF, SGP, Suffolk, 1949

27 *Owlet-Nightjar* Olympus OM-2n, 135mm Zuiko, f5.6, T32 fill-in flash, K64, Tarango Zoo, Sydney, Australia, 1981

29 *Young Long-eared Owls* Contax, 135mm Sonnar, f5.6, 1/250th, Verichrome, Norfolk, 1942

30 *Snowy Owl* SZT, Birdland, Bourton-on-the-Water, Gloucestershire, 1975
Galapagos Short-eared Owl Hasselblad, 150mm Sonnar, f11, Plus-X Pan, Galapagos, 1970

32, 33 *Little Owl* Hasselblad, 80mm Planar, f16, HSF-B, E200, Shropshire, 1981 (David Hosking)

34 *Equipment set-up* Olympus OM2-n, 50mm Zuiko, f5.6, Auto, K64, Shropshire, 1981 (David Hosking)

35 *Little Owl* (left) Contarex, 250mm Sonnar, f11, 1/250th, Pan-X, Jordan, 1963
Little Owl (right) Hasselblad, 350mm Tele-Tessar, f12.5, Braun 700, E64, South Devon, 1974 (David Hosking)

36 *Masked Owl* Olympus OM-2n, 135mm Zuiko, f11, T32, K64, Featherdale Bird Gardens, New South Wales, Australia, 1981
Spix Screech Owl SZT, London Zoo, 1970

38 *Scops Owl* SZT, London Zoo, 1972
Eastern Screech Owl SZT, Chester Zoo, Cheshire, 1976

39 *Great Horned Owl* SZT, Cricket St Thomas, Somerset, 1977
White-faced Scops Owl Hasselblad, 250mm

P1200, Suffolk, 1945

127 *Barn Owl family* (both pictures) SFC, 21cm Tessar, f8, Sashalite bulb, SGP, Norfolk, 1942
128 *Barn Owl* TPQPR, 16'' Tele-Tessar, f8, 1/500th, GIZ, Suffolk, 1933
129 *Barn Owl* SZT, Chester Zoo, Cheshire, 1971
130 *Long-eared Owl* SZT, Falconry Centre, Gloucestershire, 1979
131 *Galapagos Short-eared Owl* Contarex, 135mm, f8, 1/250th, KX, Galapagos, 1970 (David Hosking)
132 *African Marsh Owl* Hasselblad, 250mm Sonnar, f5.6, Braun 700, Agfa 50s, Zimbabwe, 1972
133 *Short-eared Owl* SZT, London Zoo, 1970
134 *Little Owl* SZT, Falconry Centre, 1980
135 *Spotted Little Owl* SZT, Essex, 1978
136 *Pharaoh Eagle Owl* SZT, Malindi, East Africa, 1976
137 *Eagle Owl* SZT, Cricket St Thomas, Somerset, 1975
138 *Abyssinian Eagle Owl* SZT, Essex, 1978
139 *Turkestan Eagle Owl* SZT, Essex, 1978 (David Hosking)

140 *Spotted Eagle Owl* SZT, Chester Zoo, Cheshire, 1977
141 *Mackinder's Eagle Owl* Hasselblad, 250mm Sonnar, f8, 1/125th, E64, Lake Baringo, Kenya, 1976
142 *Nduk Eagle Owl* SZT, London Zoo, 1981
143 *Cape Eagle Owl* SZT, Harewood Bird Garden, South Yorkshire, 1979
144 *Verreaux's Eagle Owl* Hasselblad, 500mm Tele-Tessar, f8, 1/125th, E64, Lake Baringo, Kenya, 1976
145 *Magellan Eagle Owl* SZT, Essex, 1978
146 *Great Horned Owl* SZT, Cricket St Thomas, Somerset, 1975
147 *Great Horned Owl* SZT, Chester, 1980
148 *Barking Owl* Olympus OM-2n, 300mm Zuiko, f4.5, T32 flash, K64, Burleigh Bird Sanctuary, Queensland, Australia, 1981
149 *African Wood Owl* SZT, Malindi, East Africa, 1976
150 *Powerful Owl* As page 148
151 *Collared Scops Owl* SZT, Essex, 1978
152 *Seychelles Bare-legged Scops Owl* Olympus OM-2,

135mm Zuiko, f4.5, Auto Quick 310, K64, Seychelles, 1978
153 *Eastern Screech Owl* SZT, London Zoo, 1977
154 *Vermiculated Fishing Owl* SZT, Chester Zoo, Cheshire, 1978
155 *Rufous Fishing Owl* SZT, Chester Zoo, Cheshire, 1978
156 *Burrowing Owl* SZT, London, 1981
157 *Rusty Barred Owl* SZT, Essex, 1978
158 *Spotted Wood Owl* SZT, Birdland, Bourton-on-the-Water, Gloucestershire, 1976
159 *Barred Owl* Olympus Om-2n, 100m Zuiko, f5.6, Auto, K64, Falconry Centre, Gloucestershire, 1980
160 *Northern Hawk Owl* Contax, 300mm Kilfitt, f4.5, 1/250th, KX, Finland, 1958
161 *Australian Barn Owl* Olympus OM-2n, 135mm Zuiko, f8, T32, K64, Featherdale Bird Gardens, New South Wales, Australia
162 *African Barn Owl* Hasselblad, 250mm Sonnar, f5.6, Braun 700, Agfa 50s, Zimbabwe, 1972
162 and 163 *Masked Owl* SZT, Featherdale Bird Gardens, New South Wales, Australia.

List of Scientific and English Names

This list has been adapted from that given by J. L. Peters in his *Birds of the World*, Vol. IV, published in 1940 by the Harvard University Press. Rather than retain Peters' arrangement of genera and species, for ease of reference genera (within subfamilies) are listed alphabetically, and within each genus, the species too are in alphabetical order. A further taxonomic sub-division, the sub-species or race, is occasionally mentioned in the text, and these have been added to this list. However, several species of owl with wide-ranging distributions have many sub-species, so many that to detail all known sub-species here would impossibly complicate this list: they have therefore been omitted.

CLASS: Aves

ORDER: STRIGIFORMES

FAMILY: *TYTONIDAE*
(Barn and Grass Owls)

SUBFAMILY: *PHODILINAE*
(Bay Owls)

Phodilus badius	Common Bay Owl
P. prigoginei	Congo Bay Owl

SUBFAMILY: *TYTONINAE*

GENUS: *TYTO*

Tyto alba	Common Barn Owl
T. a. affinis	African Barn Owl
T. a. delicatula	Australian Barn Owl
T. aurantia	New Britain Barn Owl
T. capensis	Common Grass Owl
T. inexpectata	Minahassa Barn Owl
T. novaehollandiae	Masked Owl
T. rosenbergii	Celebes Barn Owl
T. soumagnei	Madagascar Owl
T. tenebricosa	Sooty Owl

FAMILY: *STRIGIDAE*

SUBFAMILY: *BUBONINAE*
(Typical Owls)

GENUS: *ATHENE*

Athene blewitti	Forest Little Owl
A. brama	Spotted Little Owl
A. noctua	Little Owl

GENUS: *BUBO*

Bubo africanus	Spotted Eagle Owl
B. a. cinerascens	Abyssinian Eagle Owl
B. bubo	(Eurasian) Eagle Owl
B. b. ascalaphus	Pharaoh (Desert or Savigny's) Eagle Owl
B. b. turcomanus	Turkestan Eagle Owl
B. capensis	Cape Eagle Owl
B. c. mackinderi	Mackinder's Eagle Owl
B. coromandus	Dusky Eagle Owl
B. lacteus	Verreaux's or Milky Eagle Owl
B. leucostictus	Akun Eagle Owl
B. nipalensis	Forest Eagle Owl
B. philippensis	Philippine Eagle Owl
B. poensis	Fraser's Eagle Owl
B. p. vosseleri	Nduk Eagle Owl
B. shelleyi	Shelley's Eagle Owl
B. sumatrana	Malaysian Eagle Owl
B. virginianus	Great Horned Owl
B. v. nacurutu	Magellan Eagle Owl

GENUS: *CICCABA*

Ciccaba albitarsus	Rufous-banded Owl
C. huhula	Black-banded Owl
C. nigrolineata	Black and White Owl
C. virgata	Mottled Owl
C. woodfordii	African Wood Owl

GENUS: *GLAUCIDIUM*

Glaucidium brasilianum	Ferruginous Pygmy Owlet
G. brodiei	Collared Pygmy Owl
G. capense	Barred Owlet
G. cuculoides	Cuckoo Owlet (Barred Pygmy Owl)
G. gnoma	Northern Pygmy Owl
G. minutissimum	Least Pygmy Owl
G. passerinum	Eurasian Pygmy Owl
G. perlatum	Pearl-spotted Owlet
G. radiatum	Barred Jungle Owlet
G. siju	Cuban Pygmy Owl
G. sjostedti	Chestnut-backed Owlet
G. tephronotum	Red-chested Owlet

GENUS: *XENOGLAUX*

Xenoglaux loweryi	Long-whiskered Owlet

GENUS: *KETUPA*

Ketupa blakistoni	Blakiston's Fish Owl
K. flavipes	Tawny Fish Owl
K. ketupa	Malaysian Fish Owl
K. zeylonensis	Brown Fish Owl

GENUS: *LOPHOSTRIX*

Lophostrix cristata	Crested Owl
L. lettii	Maned Owl

GENUS: *MICRATHENE*

Micrathene whitneyi	Elf Owl

GENUS: *NINOX*

Ninox affinis	Andaman Hawk Owl
N. connivens	Barking Owl
N. jacquinoti	Solomon Islands Hawk Owl
N. meeki	Admiralty Islands Hawk Owl
N. novaeseelandiae	Boobook Owl
N. odiosa	New Britain Hawk Owl
N. perversa	Ochre-bellied Hawk Owl
N. philippensis	Philippine Hawk Owl
N. punctulata	Speckled Hawk Owl
N. rufa	Rufous Owl
N. scutulata	Oriental Hawk Owl
N. solomonis	New Ireland Hawk Owl
N. squamipila	Moluccan Hawk Owl
N. strenua	Powerful Owl
N. superciliaris	Madagascar Hawk Owl
N. theomacha	Sooty-backed Hawk Owl

GENUS: *NYCTEA*

Nyctea scandiaca	Snowy Owl

GENUS: *OTUS*

Otus albogularis	White-throated Screech Owl
O. alfredi	Flores Scops Owl
O. asio	Eastern Screech Owl
O. atricapillus	Black-capped Screech Owl
O. bakkamoena	Collared Scops Owl
O. balli	Andaman Scops Owl
O. barbarus	Santa Barbara Screech Owl
O. brookii	Rajah's Scops Owl
O. choliba	Spix or Choliba Screech Owl
O. clarkii	Bare-shanked Screech Owl
O. cooperi	Pacific Screech Owl
O. flammeolus	Flammulated Owl
O. guatemalae	Vermiculated Screech Owl
O. gurneyi	Giant Scops Owl
O. hartlaubi	São Thomé Scops Owl

O. icterorhynchus	Sandy Scops Owl	P. perspicillata	Spectacled Owl
O. ingens	Rufescent Scops Owl		
O. ireneae	Sokoke Scops Owl	GENUS: SCELOGLAUX	
O. kennicotti	Western Screech Owl	Sceloglaux albifacies	Laughing Owl (thought to be extinct)
O. lawrencii	Cuban Screech Owl		
O. leucotis	White-faced Scops Owl	GENUS: SCOTOPELIA	
O. manadensis	Celebes Scops Owl	Scotopelia bouvieri	Vermiculated Fishing Owl
O. nudipes	Puerto Rican Screech Owl	S. peli	Pel's Fishing Owl
O. podarginus	Palau Scops Owl	S. ussheri	Rufous Fishing Owl
O. roboratus	Roborate Screech Owl		
O. rufescens	Reddish Scops Owl	GENUS: SPEOTYTO	
O. rutilus	Madagascan Scops Owl	Speotyto cunicularia	Burrowing Owl
O. r. insularis	Seychelles Bare-legged Scops Owl	GENUS: SURNIA	
O. sagittatus	White-fronted Scops Owl	Surnia ulula	Northern Hawk Owl
O. scops	(Common) Scops Owl	GENUS: UROGLAUX	
O. silvicolus	Lesser Sunda Scops Owl	Uroglaux dimorpha	Papuan Hawk Owl
O. spilocephalus	Spotted Scops Owl		
O. sunia	Oriental Scops Owl	SUBFAMILY: STRIGINAE	
O. trichopsis	Spotted Screech Owl	GENUS: AEGOLIUS	
O. watsonii	Tawny-bellied Screech Owl	Aegolius acadicus	Saw-whet Owl
		A. funereus	Tengmalm's (Boreal) Owl
GENUS: PULSATRIX		A. harrisii	Buff-fronted Owl
Pulsatrix koeniswaldiana	White-chinned Owl	A. ridgwayi	Unspotted Saw-whet Owl
P. melanota	Rusty-barred (Brazilian) Owl	GENUS: ASIO	
		Asio capensis	African Marsh Owl

A. flammeus	Short-eared Owl
A. f. galapagensis	Galapagos Short-eared Owl
A. madagascariensis	Madagascar Long-eared Owl
A. otus	Long-eared Owl
A. stygius	Stygian Owl
GENUS: NESASIO	
Nesasio solomonensis	Fearful Owl
GENUS: PSEUDOSCOPS	
Pseudoscops grammicus	Jamaican Owl
GENUS: RHINOPTYNX	
Rhinoptynx clamator	Striped Owl
GENUS: STRIX	
Strix aluco	Tawny Owl
S. butleri	Hume's Wood Owl
S. hylophila	Rusty-barred Owl
S. leptogrammica	Brown Wood Owl
S. nebulosa	Great Grey Owl
S. occidentalis	Spotted Owl
S. ocellata	Mottled Wood Owl
S. rufipes	Rufous-legged Owl
S. seloputo	Spotted Wood Owl
S. uralensis	Ural Owl
S. varia	Barred Owl

Index

Least Pygmy Owl, 42
Legs, 67, 69
Little Owl, 22, 28, 31, 32–3, 34, 35, 39, 48, 50, 51, 55, 56, 62, 63, 71, 72, 73, 74, 77, 84, 85, 90, 91, 94, 97, 134
Long-eared Owl, 29, 42, 44, 53, 54, 56, 65, 67, 71, 78, 85, 97, 130
Long-whiskered Owlet, 47

Mackinder's Eagle Owl, 141
Magellan Eagle Owl, 145
Man, attitude to owls, 23–4
Masked Owl, 35, 36, 162, 163
Micrathene genus, 28, 39
Milky Eagle Owl, (Verreaux's Owl), 54, 82, 144
Miocene Period, 25–6
Mottled Owl, 38, 42
Mottled Wood Owl, 42

Nduk Eagle Owl, 142
Neck, 62
Neolithic times, owls as part of man's diet, 22
Nestboxes, 94, 97, 102–3
Nests, nesting, 78, 79, 83, 101, 103, 105
Nictitating eyelid, 61, 62, 65, 93
Nightjar, 26
Ninox genus, 42, 45, 47, 75
Northern Hawk Owl, 39, 41, 160
Northern Pygmy Owl, 41
Nyctea genus, 28

Oligocene Period, 25
Ordovican Period, 24
Oriental Hawk Owl, 45
Oriental Scops Owl, 37
Otus genus, 26, 28, 37
Owl Butterfly, 53
Owlet-nightjar, 27
Owlets, 42

Pearl-spotted Owlet, 42, 76

Pellets (castings), 71, 73, 75
Pel's Fishing Owl, 38
Pharaoh Eagle Owl, 66, 70, 136
Phodilus genus, 35, 37
Photographic equipment for owl studies, 19
Plumage, 49–55, 64, 68, 113, 117, 119
Powerful Owl, 17, 47, 60, 150
Prey, *see* Food and feeding
Printed word, owls in the, 21–2
Protostrigidae, 25
Pseudoscops genus, 42
Pulsatrix genus, 38
Pygmy Owl, 30, 41–3, 75, 77, 90
Pygmy Owlet, 28

Reddish Scops Owl, 37
Relatives of the Owls, 26–7
Rufous Fishing Owl, 38, 155
Rufous Owl, 17, 18, 47
Rusty-barred Owl, 157

Saw-whet Owl, 41
Sceloglaux genus, 28
Scops Owl, 28, 37, 38, 39, 54, 86, 99, 152
Scotopelia genus, 28, 31, 37, 38
Screech Owl, 28, 37, 38, 54
Sensory systems, 58–67
Seychelles Bare-legged Scops, 152
Short-eared Owl, 25, 28, 30, 31, 35, 42–5, 55, 56, 57, 63, 71, 80–1, 85, 88, 89, 92, 93, 97, 131, 133
Sight, *see* Eyes
Size, 99
Snowy Owl, 22, 26, 28, 30, 31, 39, 69, 70, 71, 79, 87, 88, 94, 95, 96
Sooty Owl, 35
Species of owls, 27–30; number of, 25–6
Spectacled Owl, 38, 40, 66
Speotyto genus, 25, 26, 39
Spix Owl, 36, 37
Spotted Eagle Owl, 23, 67, 88, 138, 140

Spotted Little Owl, 39, 135
Spotted Scops Owl, 37
Spotted Wood Owl, 42, 67, 158
Strigidae, 25, 27
Strigiformes, 27
Striginae, 28
Strix genus, 26, 28, 42
Stygian Owl, 42
Surnia genus, 28

Tawny Owl, 12, 15, 16, 17, 21, 24, 28, 34, 37, 42, 49, 54, 55, 58, 61, 68, 71, 75, 94, 97, 98
  breeding, 100–11
  camouflage, 100, 101
  co-existence with man, 111
  diet, 111
  habitat, 99
  hunting techniques, 111
  mobbing by other birds, 100
  nest, 101, 103, 105
  nestboxes, 102–3
  range, 99
  size, 99
  study of, 99–111
Taxonomic order, 27–30
Tengmalm's Owl, 20, 41
Turkestan Eagle Owl, 59, 139
Tyto genus, 25, 27, 28, 35

Ural Owl, 42

Vermiculated Fishing Owl, 38, 154
Vermiculated Screech Owl, 37
Verreaux's Eagle Owl, 54, 82, 144

Warning of owls' possible aggressiveness towards inquisitive humans, 107, 111
Weights of owls, 30
Western Screech Owl, 37
White-faced Scops Owl, 39
Wings, 49–51, 53, 56, 57, 117, 119, 120, 124
Wood Owl, 28, 42